About the Marijke Method™

"Thank you Marijke for sharing your incredible gift."

"I always know that Marijke will clarify what the true issues are – she is our primary health care provider."

"Marijke's strong science background enhanced by her medical intuition and communication skills makes her a unique healer".

"…a knowledgeable and educated healer."

"I don't understand how she does what she does, it's magic really."

"She reads me like a book."

"This is the method that I've been wanting for years."

"She not only provides sound judgment and healthy nutritional advice but she is a guide for how we want to live our life now and in the future."

"No one has ever been able to help me in this area (except for you). Thank you for being you and for following your intuition."

"Marijke is a joy to study with! I was astounded by the amount of information I took in."

"Marijke is an intuitive healer who addresses the person spiritually, emotionally, mentally, and physically."

"I have worked with Marijke for over two decades…her insights have guided me through difficulties of which conventional medicine could only treat symptoms."

"There are natural doctors and healers…and then there's Marijke."

"It's amazing how in just a few minutes she knows where the problem is."

"I have trusted Marijke with my health care for years."

I am reaching out to the person that I BELIEVE has the intuition, knowledge, experience and discretion to truly help me.

"No matter what I come in with, every time I leave her office there's a major shift."

"Marijke has an amazing and beautiful positive attitude – I feel better just being around her."

*"I always tell my friends that I believe in Marijke like I believe in God. And I mean it.
I'd been suffering from severe insomnia for almost a year…Marijke took a good look at me and said it was caused by my iron supplement. The next night I slept like a baby and have been ever since!"*

"I was immediately referred to you for guidance and knew instantly I had the right person".

HEALING PEOPLE
The Marijke Method™
by Marijke van de Water

Balboa Press books may be ordered through booksellers or by contacting:

Balboa Press
A Division of Hay House
1663 Liberty Drive
Bloomington, IN 47403
www.balboapress.com
1-(877) 407-4847

Because of the dynamic nature of the Internet, any web addresses or links contained in this book may have changed since publication and may no longer be valid. The views expressed in this work are solely those of the author and do not necessarily reflect the views of the publisher, and the publisher hereby disclaims any responsibility for them.

The author of this book does not dispense medical advice or prescribe the use of any technique as a form of treatment for physical, emotional, or medical problems without the advice of a physician, either directly or indirectly. The intent of the author is only to offer information of a general nature to help you in your quest for emotional and spiritual well-being. In the event you use any of the information in this book for yourself, which is your constitutional right, the author and the publisher assume no responsibility for your actions.

Any people depicted in stock imagery provided by Thinkstock are models, and such images are being used for illustrative purposes only.

Certain stock imagery © Thinkstock.

ISBN: 978-1-4525-6088-5 (sc)
ISBN: 978-1-4525-6089-2 (e)

Library of Congress Control Number: 2012919280

Printed in the United States of America

Balboa Press rev. date: 10/12/2012

This book is dedicated to the thousands of people who entrusted me with their health care over so many years. You have all gifted me more than you will ever know …knowledge, healing, compassion and spirit. May it be returned to you tenfold!

Marijke

Contents

5. THE MARIJKE METHOD™

6. TESTING ORGAN POINTS AND BODY SYSTEMS

8. REFERENCE GUIDE TO HEALTH CONDITIONS

9. SUPPLEMENTS, HOMEOPATHY & HERBS

APPENDICES

RECOMMENDED READING

ABOUT MARIJKE

Introduction

This is the book I said I would never write. Patients, clients, customers and friends alike frequently asked if this book would ever be written. In 2008, I had published *Healing Horses: Their Way!*, a dense and information-packed book on equine nutrition and natural healing. Naturally, the expectation was that human nutrition would be my next project. However, the challenges of taking on the human health industry - which doesn't much care about food - to affect any kind of change, seemed like a prodigious task. My standpoint on the relationship between health and nutrition paled beside every barbeque, birthday party and fund-raiser (even for cancer) forever serving the typical North American diet: hot dogs; nachos; baked goods; big bread sandwiches; cheese; pizzas; ice-cream; deep-fried everything and pounds of sugar. Frankly, I had a better chance of helping horses!

What I did feel compelled to do was to write a book on helping people heal with kinesiology - energy testing by using muscle strength to diagnose health imbalances, and formulate health programs. After over two decades of private practice working with both people and horses, I had developed a unique and specialized method of energy testing for establishing comprehensive and successful health programs for many health conditions. Two chapters into the first draft I realized that I could not effectively teach this method without the reader or student establishing a basic foundation of knowledge in nutrition, body function, physiology and the effects of diet and nutrition on disease. So there it was – my user-friendly handbook on kinesiology quickly mushroomed to include extensive information on nutrition. (I am fully aware of the benefits of surrendering…)

I started out by making solid statements about nutrition and health, but as the book progressed I gleefully began to enjoy my new soapbox from which I could deliver a passionate and vehement assertion that food not only causes most diseases but is also capable of healing them. As is so often the case when you put something into writing, I achieved a renewed clarity by outlining the logic, the criteria and the arguments validated by years of nutritional science. It also explained the thousands of successes that I witnessed for over two decades through guiding and counseling people within my role as a nutritional therapist and healer. In the process, I repeatedly refuted the commonly held belief system in mainstream medicine that disease is a random event over which we have no control; that we are helpless victims swallowed up by the giant wheel of modern high-tech medicine; and that the very diseases that high-tech medicine promises to fix have mostly been caused by a high-tech world. There is no therapy as capable as nutritional therapy to silence the critics of natural medicine once and for all. Nutritional medicine is a documented, viable and effective healing modality that is still – despite modern dietary research, the advent of integrated health practices, and the emergence of thousands of health food stores - absolutely undervalued. Let's put it where it rightly belongs – smack dab in the middle of primary health care!

But knowledge isn't enough - I knew that, in order to be of value, **Healing People: The Marijke Method**™ *needed to translate both knowledge and experience into a practical method that every person could use for healing.* Every healing modality, no matter how impressive, must first recognize the unique "blueprint" that makes each of us special; the same blueprint that determines our individual underlying causes of unwellness. In this way we avoid treating labels and diseases in place of treating the whole person. It is here that combining the art of kinesiology with the science of nutritional knowledge excels. *The Marijke Method*™ is a simple yet powerful healing technique that takes the guesswork out of the health equation and replaces it with insight, awareness and strategies for recovery. It is practical, sensible, effective and really fun!

This is the book I really, really needed to write. Thank you for reading it on your journey to spectacular health…

Marijke

Chapter 1

THE HEALTHY DIET
- And the Not So Healthy Diet -

"No illness which can be treated by diet
should be treated by any other means"
......**Maimonides, 1158 AD**

Food affects every health condition. Food has a direct and profound effect on everything from digestion, headaches, skin problems, immune disorders, heart disease, arthritis, and cancer, to hormones, energy levels, stress, depression, anxiety, and mental and emotional disorders. Diet, food allergies, food intolerances and nutrient deficiencies control our state of health. Even when disturbances are accompanied by significant emotional and mental imbalances, the proper care of the physical body has a major influence on recovery. Too many times I have watched patients with chronic illnesses embark on a long journey of emotional healing while their health continues to deteriorate because the toxicity and nutritional requirements of the physical body have been ignored.

Considering the average North American diet, the condition of our food supply, and that most people are deficient in multiple nutrients, it is no surprise that the very foods that should sustain us are poisoning us.

Therapeutic nutrition is the therapy that is given the least value by medical and holistic practitioners alike, and yet, in my opinion, it has the potential to heal more conditions than any other modality. If I had to choose only one therapy (and I am glad I don't) it would be - hands down - diet and nutritional therapy.

Nutrition is so much more than the prescription of a multi vitamin or the recommendation of random vitamins and minerals. It is much more than routine eating. It is much more than eating "sensibly" from the five food groups. It is much more than just food allergies. And, it is even more than a colon cleanse!

What constitutes a healthy diet is not a secret. Scientific studies, journals, publications and text books abound with information on what is good for us and what is not good for us. Not to mention our own inner knowing as to what makes us feel good. So why can't we seem to get it straight? Why is it that food continues to make us confused and crazy? There are plenty of reasons.

a) The volume and mass marketing of junk food is everywhere we go - if everybody else is eating it, it must be okay…

b) Junk food is physically addictive…did you know that? The excess of sugar, salt and fat routinely added to processed foods reconfigure our taste buds. In time, we are only satisfied by the foods that contain these excesses, and we can no longer appreciate or enjoy naturally occurring flavours of unprocessed foods, fruits and vegetables.

c) Money rules over health - economic realities dictate that food companies manufacture what sells.

d) We are inundated with information and confused by hundreds of diet plans, conflicting statistics and media reporting that bombard our kitchens every day.

e) We shop and drive-through instead of hunting and gathering; many people don't even know where food really comes from let alone how it's processed. We don't even know if any of our food sources are sustainable.

f) There is a chronic lack of public information linking diet to disease. Instead, we hear such nonsense as "french fries are a good source of Vitamin C…caffeine prevents diabetes… sugar gives you energy…" Or the ludicrous misinformation that a single panacea will cure all our ails and we can then eat whatever we want: case in point this year is the excessive media attention on Vitamin D as a miracle cancer preventative among other inflated health benefits. Nowhere, however, are we reminded that vitamin D is a fat-soluble vitamin that, when taken in excess, can be destructive to the cardiovascular system.

g) We are relying on information from a food industry that knows very little about health, and from a health industry that knows very little about food.

h) There is an inexcusable lack of dietary and nutritional knowledge within the medical industry. Are they still passing out coffee and donuts in the chemotherapeutic waiting rooms?

i) We have become disconnected. We have lost our connection to Mother Nature, to the "energetics" of food and to our instinct about what foods our bodies need.

So, before we learn how to identify food problems and therapeutic diets - for ourselves and for others - we need to take a look at some solid information about the food that we eat, the food that we shouldn't eat and the food that will help us live a long and healthy life. And if, after you read this book, you still choose to eat a toxic diet you can't say you didn't know better.

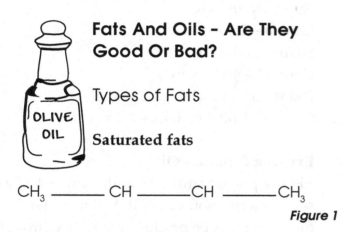

Fats And Oils - Are They Good Or Bad?

Types of Fats

Saturated fats

$$CH_3 \text{———} CH \text{———} CH \text{———} CH_3$$

Figure 1

A saturated fat is a fat which is solid at room temperature and is stable in the presence of high heat and strong light and it has a high melting point. All meat fat is saturated, including butter, whole milk products, beef and poultry. Plant sources of saturated fats include palm oil and coconut oil. Saturated fats are usually greasy in texture. (What makes a saturated fat saturated is that the carbon atoms are connected by a single bond rather than carbon-carbon double bonds. Instead the second bond is used by a hydrogen atom. Saturation refers to the fact that the fat is saturated with hydrogen atoms. The single bonds don't break apart easily and allow for a high degree of stability - saturated fats are not easily denatured by high heat or light.)

Contrary to popular opinion, saturated fats, because of their stability, are not that bad for your health. Eggs, poultry and coconuts don't cause disease, but over-consumption does.

So; don't eat poultry skin, don't smother everything in butter, don't leave your steak untrimmed, don't eat fatty sausage meat or processed meats, and don't dip your morning toast into the bacon grease. All meat should be eaten fresh, lean and "light".

Polyunsaturated fats

$$CH_2 \text{═══} CH \text{═══} CH \text{═══} CH_2$$

Figure 2

These fats are unsaturated – in other words, they contain fewer hydrogen atoms thus they are not fully saturated with hydrogen, making more bonds available to the carbon-carbon connections. (Thus, many of the carbon-carbon bonds in these fats are now double bonds, rather than a single one such as is the case with saturated fats. What these double bonds mean from a biochemical perspective is that unsaturated oils are liquid at room temperature and have a lower melting point. They are therefore very reactive and unstable in the presence of heat, light and processing, and combine easily with oxygen causing rancidity.) If they are not kept cool or not stored in dark bottles they easily denature (changing their natural properties) and become toxic to our health. Polyunsaturated fats include fish oils, flax seed oil, hemp seed oil, nut oils, corn oil, sunflower seed oil, and all vegetable oils.

Essential Fatty Acids

These are a special type of polyunsaturate essential to life and good health. They are found mainly in the brain, adrenal, inner ear and reproductive glands. There are 2 different types of essential fatty acids: linolenic acid (omega

3) and linoleic acid (omega 6). Both of them must be provided in the diet since the body cannot manufacture essential fatty acids on its own.

Omega 3 is provided by leafy greens, blue-green algae (spirulina), flax seeds, hemp seeds, sesame seeds, walnuts, soybeans and cold water fish such as salmon because they feed on algae. Omega 3's convert into GLA (gamma linolenic acid) which then converts into healthy prostaglandins that support the liver, increase metabolism, benefit the cardio-vascular system, prevent blood clots, help skin conditions, balance reproductive hormones, improve mental health and improve immune deficiencies, including food allergies. They also reduce inflammation, asthma, and arthritis. Even though EFA's are extremely beneficial they cannot override a diet full of bad fats.

Omega 6's are found in meat, eggs, nuts, beans and almost all vegetable oils. Excess omega 6 converts into unhealthy prostaglandins that not only compete with the health benefits of omega 3's but also cause inflammation leading to a variety of disorders such as heart conditions, blood clots, arthritis, osteoporosis, inflammation, mood disorders, obesity and cancer. Consumption of sugar and grains also encourages the conversion of omega 6 fats into pro-inflammatory prostaglandins.

While both of these essential fatty acids are important, it is the ratio in which they are eaten that is critical to our health. While the optimum ratio in our diets should be 2:1 to 4:1

omega 6 to omega 3, the typical Western diet is often in excess of 30:1! This disease-causing excess is caused by the daily consumption of cheap vegetable oils, mainly found in processed foods. Look at these ratios and check out your salad dressings, baked goods, corn chips, etc. etc. etc.

Canola – 2:1
Soybean oil – 7:1
Corn oil – 46:1 (wow!)
Peanut oil – no Omega 3's at all
Sunflower oil – no Omega 3's at all

Evening Primrose Oil
EPO is polyunsaturated and, similar to flax seed, is a rich source of GLA. But the GLA in flax seed must be produced from LA through a series of chemical conversions. Not everyone is able to make this conversion, especially people with high fat diets, high sugar diets, liver congestion, alcohol consumption, obesity, poor immunity and metabolic syndrome. This means that evening primrose oil is often a more effective and beneficial supplement than flax seed or hemp seed.

Monounsaturated Fats

$$CH_2 = CH - CH_2 = CH_2$$

Figure 3

A monounsaturated fat is a fat molecule that contains one pair of carbon atoms connected by a double bond, rather than multiple double bonds as is the case with polyunsaturates. The monounsaturation of this molecule gives it more stability than the polyunsaturates making these fats relatively safe choices for cooking and heating. It is generally accepted knowledge that monounsaturated fats are healthier than both saturated and most poly-unsaturated fats and oils.

Monounsaturated fats are found in nuts, av-ocados, grapeseed oil, sesame oil, and olive oil. Olive oil is a natural anti-oxidant, anti-inflammatory and is beneficial for the heart, liver and gallbladder. Grapeseed oil is a light, nutty flavoured oil helpful for the prevention of heart disease, cancer, eyesight problems, arthritis, poor circulation and allergies.

Trans-fatty acids

"Trans" fatty acid - Figure 4

"Cis" fatty acid - Figure 5

Unfortunately, the modern Western diet contains a lot of hydrogenated oils. The process of hydrogenation allows food manufacturers to start with a cheap, poor quality, polyun-saturated liquid vegetable oil (high in omega 6) and harden it so they can pour it into a container and spread it like margarine, or use it in processed foods. Oils that are hydroge-nated have been subjected to high heat and pressure with hydrogen gas. The hydrogen atoms saturate the oil molecule, destroying the double bonds, raising the melting point and thus the oil "hardens" like a saturated fat. Unfortunately, this unnatural processing

bonds the hydrogen atoms to opposite sides of the molecule (trans), rather than on the same side (cis) as is the case with a natural saturated fat found in meat.

This change in molecular structure is drastic. The liver, heart and brain have no idea how to use these "artificial" fats for any of their vital functions. Trans-fats are implicated in heart disease, strokes, cancer, diabetes, obe-sity, liver diseases, mental health disorders and degenerative diseases.

In other words, *trans-fatty acids are poisons.*

Trans-fatty acids are easy to avoid if you don't eat processed foods. Margarine, short-ening, baked goods such as cookies, muffins, pastries, cakes, pies, and donuts, cake mixes, pancake mixes, pasta dinners, processed ce-reals, corn chips and potato chips are all ex-amples of trans-fat laden foods. Read the la-bels.

Free Radicals

All atoms are made up of electrons, small sub-atomic particles that dance around at the speed of light and are normally found in pairs, which they like. In fact, when unpaired they are so obsessed with finding a mate that they will steal another electron from wherev-er they can, including another electron pair. (Sound familiar?) So when the hydrogen at-oms (electrons) in a polyunsaturated double bond become exposed to heat, oxygen or light, they become very excited and split off leaving behind a lonely and desperate mate. This unpaired electron now steals a partner from wherever it can, leaving another electron unpaired. This sets off a chain reaction that can go through thousands of cycles all the while tearing apart tissues, impairing biochemical functions and producing toxic substances. This insidious process damages cellular DNA, causing disease to the cardiovascular system, immune system, skin, connective tissue, brain and nervous system, and ultimately causes cancer. Recent studies have shown these degenerative diseases to be of oxidative origin.

$$CH_3 - \overset{\overset{\displaystyle H}{|}}{C} = \overset{\overset{\displaystyle H}{|}}{C} - \overset{\overset{\displaystyle H}{|}}{\underset{\bullet}{C}} - CH_3$$

Unpaired free electron

Free Radical - Figure 6

Other causes of free radical damage include smoking, excess alcohol intake, stress and excessive aerobic exercise, for example distance running, due to the volume of oxygen intake. Strength training (anaerobic) and sprinting are better choices.

So if these polyunsaturated double-bonded oils cause us nothing but trouble, why don't we eliminate them out of the diet completely?

a) A certain number of free radicals are necessary to maintain health – they facilitate thousands of normal chemical reactions.

b) Essential fatty acids attract oxygen to the cells producing energy and preventing diseases that thrive in an oxygen-free environment: cancer; cardiovascular disease; arthritis; obesity and aging.

c) Essential fatty acids, already dangerously deficient in the Western diet, are absolutely necessary for sustaining good health and life itself.

We cannot avoid all polyunsaturates. They are essential. The key is that we need to avoid any polyunsaturated oils that have been exposed to heat, light or oxygen.

Cooking tips for oils
a) Don't cook with any type of vegetable oils or other polyunsaturates – it is one of the worst things that you can do for your health! The only oils that are safe to heat for cooking purposes are those oils with a high smoke point, in other words, those oils that remain intact when heated up: butter; coconut oil; olive oil and grapeseed oil.

b) Never eat deep-fried foods or oil heated in the absence of oxygen. Not only does this produce trans-fatty acids, but deep-fried foods are a major source of other toxic oxidative and polymer substances that are a major health hazard. In commercial operations the same batch of denatured oil is often kept at a high temperature for days. Say good-bye to the French fries.

c) Add water to your fry pan first and don't add any oil until the vegetables have been added. This protects the oil from over-heating and from damaging oxidation.

d) Cook fish with very little heat – poached, lightly baked or steamed.

e) Make "better butter" – 50% butter and 50% olive oil or grapeseed oil. It will spread easily and still be beneficial for your health.

f) And better yet, instead of eating a lot of extracted oils, eat the foods that the oils come from and let Mother Nature protect these oils from heat, light and oxygen naturally in their whole state. She will also provide built-in anti-oxidant protection along with a bounty of nutrients. Eat fish, flax seed, hemp seed, sunflower seeds, sesame seeds, vegetables and spirulina. Our bodies were never intended to eat large quantities of concentrated oils, never mind the toxic, processed, denatured ones. How do we know this? Because fatty liver disease is the number one liver disease and 600,000 people in North America don't have a gallbladder. (Oh, and by the way, people with gallbladder problems have trouble making decisions.)

Anti-Oxidants

Anti-Oxidants are substances that neutralize the free electrons by donating an electron themselves to pair them up again. In other words, they restore order to electron chaos thus preventing DNA damage and degeneration. Effective and common anti-oxidants include vitamin E, vitamin C, alpha-lipoic acid, glutathione, beta-carotene, coenzyme Q10 and selenium. Most fruits and vegetables are packed with anti-oxidants, particularly berries, broccoli, garlic, tomatoes, spinach, grapes, carrots, and spirulina. And because fruits and vegetables cause no oxidation themselves, their anti-oxidant properties are completely available to "mop" up the damage from other stressors. Fruits and veg-

etables should be eaten in excess every day.

A note of caution: too many anti-oxidant supplements over a long period of time can actually cause fatigue as cells become deprived of energy-producing oxygen. Use supplements only as required and rely on your food for your nutrition. Everything in moderation…

Our bodies were never intended to ingest concentrated oils of any kind; fatty liver disease is the number one liver disease and 600,000 people in North America don't have a gallbladder.

The Fish-Coconut Story

Now we know that fish contains polyunsaturated oils and that coconuts are saturated. So why do you think the primary diet in the Arctic is fish-based and that coconut trees grow in the tropics? As we recall, polyunsaturated oils contain double bonds which are highly reactive to light – in fact they store sunlight – while saturated fats, with their absence of double bonds, are non-reactive to light and have no light-storing properties. The primary location for the storage of any kind of body fat is underneath the skin in the subcutaneous fat layer. Thus, when stored polyunsaturated fats are exposed to sunlight and heat the obvious chemical changes cause free radicals, degeneration and DNA damage, leaving us susceptible to cancer, especially skin cancer. Stored saturated fats like coconut fat, or even meat fat for that matter, protect the body from sunlight damage since their bonds are extremely stable.

The Inuit diet in the far North consists mainly of polyunsaturated and essential fatty acids derived from fish. These fats store sunlight and provide them with "sunlight" energy during long seasons of darkness. The Inuit fish diet protects them from light-deprived health conditions such as winter depression, mental dysfunction, poor immunity, bone and teeth problems, deformities and muscle weakness. Down South, the indigenous tropical diet consists of fewer fats, but primarily saturated fats, like coconut. Even wild plant foods in the tropics contain more saturated fats than in the North. (And plants in the moderate climates of North America have more polyunsaturates.) When the sunlight beats down in the tropics, the saturated fat skin layer serves to protect people from exposure, DNA damage and skin cancer.

Does the sun really cause cancer? Or is it the trans-fatty French fries, polyunsaturated corn chips or oily muffins you eat before you go outside? What do you think?

 When in Rome, do as the Romans do. If the Inuit ate coconuts instead of fish they would die; if the Guatemalans ate primarily fish oils in the hot sun they would combust.

What this means for you, wherever you live is this:
Don't eat an abundance of polyunsaturated fats or any oil supplements in the summer time - including flax seeds, hemp seeds, fish, etc. – keep those for the darker winter months. Eat more saturated fats in the summer time to protect yourself from excessive light and heat. (Isn't that what we instinctively do with summer barbeques?) Your body's own wisdom also assumes that you are more active in the summer time and will have an easier time burning off fats.

In the winter time, eat fewer saturates and more fish, nuts and seeds to help prevent light deprived conditions, including SAD (seasonal affective disorder), aka depression.

Oh yes, and don't forget to use coconut oil for a suntan lotion - all the chemicals in sunscreen are absorbed through the skin, putting you at risk for - you guessed it - cancer. Coconut oil has the added benefit of hydrating the skin and boosting collagen, the support structure for your skin. Sunscreen chemicals are powerful free radical generators, causing cellular damage. Most chemical sunscreens contain compounds such as avobenzone, benzophenone, ethylhexyl salicylate and lastly, oxybenzone, one of the most powerful free radical generators known! It is used in industrial processes as a free radical generator to initiate chemical reactions.

Many of these chemicals are also estrogenic, thus causing problems with sexual development and all the health problems that accompany excess hormone levels. Furthermore, these are synthetic chemicals that are foreign to the human body and therefore accumulate in body fat stores. Over the past decade, many scientists studying cancer have come to consistent conclusions:

that the use of sunscreen chemicals is increasing the incidence of cancer and that sunshine may actually decrease human cancer rates and improve our health. Let's put the responsibility where it belongs… on diet and chemicals, not on Father Sun.

Fats, Oils & Cancer

It is often said the health industry doesn't know anything about food, and the food industry doesn't know anything about health.

Cancer is on the rise. Why? Because we continue to believe that cancer is caused by a deficiency of radiation therapy and chemotherapeutic drugs. And all of our well-intended and hard-earned charity money goes toward researching big pharma treatment plans, rather than the identification of underlying causes. In fact, health supplements and dietary strategies are mostly discouraged as a complement to mainstream protocols, presumably because they might interfere with toxic treatment therapies. How sensible is that?

Several years ago I did a presentation for a breast cancer support group at a local hospital. Approximately 50 people attended and, for the most part, were hungry for some kind of knowledge – any kind of knowledge really – that would help them better understand their condition and what to do about it. I was appalled at the absolute lack of knowledge that every single one of these women and men (yes men get breast cancer too) had about the effect of food on their health. All but one of them had been through the usual mainstream treatment programs, and not one of them had been counselled on the benefits of diet, exercise, nutrition and general lifestyle. And most of them were overweight, an absolute risk factor for cancer. The one lady who had opted out of traditional treatment was pursuing a "macrobiotic" diet and the rest of the group nearly lynched her for refusing medical intervention.

So let's get this straight, whether you are in a support group or not. Cancer is caused by (in order):

1) Smoking
2) Diet – excess fat, sugar and calories; and a deficiency of fruit, vegetables and fibre.
3) Chronic inflammation as caused by bacteria, viruses, and infections. Chronic inflammation releases powerful oxidants.
4) Environmental chemicals and drugs.

The most successful therapy for cancer is diet and nutritional therapy. An appropriate and healthy diet will even detoxify you from the damages of smoking (after you quit) and chemical exposure. It will also protect you from disease-causing pathogens: bacteria and viruses prefer unhealthy terrain.

The trans-fatty acids and free radicals (as caused by the chemically altered and processed oils from seeds and vegetables) cause cancer by interfering with oxygen use in the cells and infusing them with toxic material. All cancer cells have depressed oxygen consumption and a concentration of debris which the cell cannot cleanse because it lacks sufficient energy.

Fats and oils present the body with major challenges due to physical incompatibility. Fats are water-insoluble. This means that fats must be emulsified: broken down by water-soluble enzymes, in order to make them digestible and to facilitate their absorption. This is accomplished with bile salts, produced from cholesterol in the liver and stored in the gallbladder. Large fat molecules and/or those that are not well dissolved don't enter the bloodstream; instead these fats directly enter into the lymphatic system and therein we have a dangerous situation. The lymph system is the main line of defense against bacteria, yeast, and viruses (which cause inflammation), foreign debris, and cancerous cells. Lymphocytes stored in the nodes destroy foreign invaders which the lymph vessels then remove. The presence of trans-fats, free radicals and excess fats and oils congest and degenerate these lymph organs seriously compromising the immune system. Thus the intake of excess and/or unhealthy fats and oils is a number one cause of cancer. Take special note with breast cancer – the breast is very full of lymph ducts, nodes and vessels. Increasing numbers of studies link high fat diets to increased risk of various cancers: particularly breast, colon, prostate, pancreas, and ovary. Fat cells also produce estrogen, the excess of which is a direct cause of breast cancer. All cancer cells contain fatty materials which cripple all of the cell's functions; healthy cells are completely free of fatty material.

You can blame the environment if you want but the internal environment rules all.

Fats, Oils, Heart Attacks, Strokes – and Possibly Cholesterol

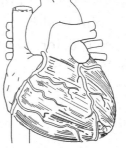

...smoking, obesity, eating fat, eating sugar, drinking beer, sedentary lifestyle, fatty liver...

Cardiovascular disease (CVD) includes heart attacks and strokes and is caused by blocked arteries. This blockage is caused by damage to the inside of the arteries and is known as artherosclerosis. It is a degenerative condition marked by fat deposits that adhere to the blood vessel wall linings. These fat deposits narrow the artery walls, creating turbulence, which then favors the clumping of blood. Blood pressure rises, which increases clotting. The consequences of narrowed arteries are circulation problems, senility and eventually heart attacks and strokes. Because the fat deposits contain cholesterol, medical treatment has focused on forcing the body to eliminate excess cholesterol in hopes of decreasing plaque formation. There is a problem with this approach: it does not address the underlying cause, which is the degeneration and damage to the blood vessel in the first place. Fatty deposits contain both saturated and unsaturated fatty acids. The role of these dietary fats, including trans-fatty acids and free radicals, is the number one villain in tissue damage and degeneration. Once the damage has been done, the liver sends in a repair team in which cholesterol is the major player. It makes absolute sense – cholesterol is very sticky and hard and makes a perfect "tire patch". It is clear, therefore, that the answer to the prevention and treatment of CVD is not accomplished by an attack on the "tire patch" with toxic medications. It is accomplished by repairing the underlying damage through diet changes and appropriate supplements – see Chapter 7.

Heart disease is not caused by high levels of cholesterol. In fact, over 50% of heart attack fatalities have normal cholesterol levels. Does that make cholesterol an accurate indicator of heart disease? Obviously not. Why would a healthy body turn one of its own hormones against itself? Cholesterol is an important hormone required for cell structure, nerve cells, brain function, synthesizing reproductive hormones, vitamin D, bile production, AND is important for fat digestion and absorption. So by reducing cholesterol levels, drug therapy encourages the mal-digestion of fats - the very foods that cause the problems in the first place. This makes about as much sense as handing out coffee and donuts (laden with trans-fats) in the medical waiting room!

While animal products are the only foods that contain cholesterol, eighty percent of the total body's requirements are actually manufactured by the liver itself. So-called "bad" cholesterol (LDL) carries fats to the repair site, while so-called "good" cholesterol" HDL removes it. HDL travels from the liver to the arteries to scavenge the unhealthy cholesterol (LDL) from the blood vessel walls when the LDL is no longer needed. This is what high cholesterol levels mean: the liver's defense mechanism is alive and well BUT both the liver and the cardiovascular system are in serious need of repair. They both need to be decongested of their "fatty" tissues and the damage to the arteries needs to be repaired through diet and exercise.

Fats and the Liver

The liver is the largest organ in the body, it weighs 3 to 5 pounds and requires a tremendous amount of the body's total energy to function. It is the main site of fat decongestion and metabolism. When the liver is overburdened it stores fats in the form of triglycerides. High triglyceride levels cause problems because they saturate the blood taking up valuable space that should be used to transport nutrients, hormones and enzymes. Fatty liver and impaired liver function due to the excess intake of dietary fats and sugars is common. Fatty liver - also caused by excess alcohol consumption - is known as liver sclerosis. Because the liver is responsible for over 500 different functions, fatty liver can detrimentally affect almost any condition in the body, especially: immunity, viral and bacterial infections; hepatitis, inflammatory conditions, arthritis, cancer, heart disease, skin problems, energy levels, sugar and protein metabolism, nutrient storage, cholesterol production and the detoxification of toxins and chemicals.

Impaired liver function therefore causes kidney stress, as the kidneys have to filter more toxins and debris that would normally be efficiently processed by a healthy liver. For this reason kidney problems should also be associated with the intake of unhealthy dietary fats. Fatty liver is also a sign that insulin levels are high leading to metabolic disorders including insulin resistance, obesity and diabetes.

A fatty liver contributes to heart disease. The toxins, fats and excessive waste material make it difficult to remove small fat globules circulating in the blood stream. These globules will eventually adhere to the blood vessel walls and damage them. The heart is particularly sensitive to these damages of unhealthy fats because, unlike the other body organs which use sugar for energy, the heart must metabolize fat for energy. A congested liver is also capable of obstructing adequate blood flow to the heart. Abdominal or "belly" fat is associated with heart disease and is a sign that the liver is plugged with fat and no longer able to burn its own fat storage deposits let alone burn excess body fats which ultimately damage the arteries, including the coronary arteries.

Fatty liver disease is the number one liver disease in North America; and yet a healthy liver contains no fat at all.

Fats and the Brain

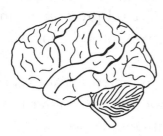 About two-thirds of your brain is composed of fats. Neurons in the brain are specialized brain nerve cells that communicate with each other via neurotransmitters, which are specialized chemicals. Their membranes are composed of a thin layer of fats. Myelin, which is the protective sheath that covers these neurons, is composed of 70% fat. These brain fats require the essential fatty acids omega 3 and omega 6 to maintain their integrity and to allow oxygen, blood sugar and nutrients entry into the brain. They also allow metabolic waste products to exit, so the brain cells won't become polluted. Brain deficiencies of essential fatty acids are linked to poor memory, depression, anxiety, brain allergies, schizophrenia, hyperactivity, attention deficit and senility. Eat your brain food – fish and flax seeds…

Unfortunately the structure of these fatty acids can be compromised by stress, infections, excess alcohol, excess sugar, nutrient deficiencies, and the damages of trans-fatty acids and rancid fats. Trans-fatty acids invade these brain cell membranes, including the myelin sheath, and degenerate the neurons by displacing the natural oils. This affects the brain's electrical activities and interferes with neuron communication, thus diminishing mental performance.

The biggest problem however, may be excess body fat. Fat cells secrete a variety of substances that cause inflammation, including inflammation of the brain which impairs learning and memory and contributes to Alzheimer's, dementia and senility. Studies have indicated that overweight people as young as 40 experience brain atrophy and a rapid decline in brain function.

Fat cells actually increase in size rather than in number. As they become bigger, they produce hormones called cytokines. Cytokines release proteins that regulate immunity, but can also promote inflammation when in excess. When fat cells become larger, they leak or burst, releasing cellular debris and toxins which the immune system must then scavenge. This process generates more cytokines, an excess of which causes systemic inflammation. We now have an understanding of how excess weight causes inflammation.

What Does All This Mean?

It means that in the typical Western diet nearly every processed food you eat contains concentrated, rancid, oxidized or damaged fats. And every unprocessed food you eat is eaten with some kind of oil or fat. Why must we soak everything in oil or fat? Think about French fries, potato chips, potato salad, corn chips, cream sauces, dips on vegetables, oil dressings on salads, oils in the fry pan, hollandaise on the eggs, shortening in the cookies, vegetable oils in crackers and bread, deep-fried fish, and meat fried in fat and then served in gravy. Your body doesn't stand a chance. Take a look at your next meal and see if you are eating fat with your food or food with your fat.

The normal digestion of fat yields fatty acids which we use for energy. If fat digestion is incomplete or compromised, it creates toxic acids instead; substances such as acetones and acetylacetic acid. Acidic body systems contribute to a host of diseases, affecting all body systems.

Pull the fats, cook with water and fire and use food, rather than oil for your supply of essential fatty acids. And try tasting your food

- real food. You will come to appreciate the goodness and nourishment that each natural food has to offer.

Catch your health problems while they are still in the energy field and before they have manifested in the physical body. Don't wait for a clinical diagnosis from the medical profession. Once a disease has begun to manifest physically it requires a lot more effort to overcome. Start now!

Carbohydrates – the Bane of the Modern Diet

Carbohydrates are the most common source of energy in living organisms, with proteins and fats used less frequently. Dietary carbohydrates, both simple and complex, are also one of the most common causes of many modern diseases. The two main forms of carbohydrates are a) simple sugars, such as fructose from fruit and lactose from milk, and b) starches which are found in starchy vegetables: grains; rice; potatoes; breads; cereals and legumes. The body breaks carbohydrates into smaller units of sugar called glucose, which are then absorbed into the bloodstream and used for energy by muscles and organs, including the brain. Simple sugars almost always contain refined sugars and contain very few nutrients such as vitamins and minerals. Daily food examples of simple carbohydrates include fruits, fruit juice, milk, honey and sugar. White sugar is refined and stripped of all trace elements, vitamins, and enzymes, thus the sugar itself becomes difficult for the body to process. Therefore, the body must release large quantities of nutrients to convert sugar into energy, which in turn causes acid formation. Sugar should be considered an anti-nutrient as it robs the body of nutrition rather than providing it.

Complex carbohydrates are always derived from plants and the simple sugars in them are bound together into a chain. They are usually packed with nutrients as well as fibre, slowing down the absorption of sugars into the bloodstream and therefore helping to regulate blood sugar disorders. Examples of complex carbohydrates include wheat bran, brown rice, oatmeal and dried beans. However - and here is where the trouble begins - refined carbohydrates are produced when whole plants (especially wheat) are ground, pounded, puffed, flaked, rolled and beat into submission so we can use it as a processed food. They are stripped of all their nutrients including the fibre. The end result is a concentrate that rapidly converts into sugar, which is highly digestible, with rapid absorption into the blood stream leading to a number of health problems. This rate of absorption is known as the Glycemic Index and is used to determine how damaging a particular sugar can be. On the other hand, if grains or beans remain in their whole form the conversion of starches into sugars is very slow, reducing the Glycemic Index thus preventing sugar-related diseases. As well, some starches with a fibrous shell convert into sugars so slowly that they reach the large colon before being digested and are fermented there into volatile fatty acids/energy. These are called resistant starches and include beans, long-grain brown rice, barley, bulgar and quinoa. These starches can be of great benefit to the large colon by increasing nutrient absorption, improving glucose tolerance, increasing satiety (feeling full longer), lowering blood fats, regulating bowel movements and balancing the ecosystem through promoting friendly bacteria and suppressing toxins. Therefore, these starches are often classified as fibre. However, one person's meat is another person's poison; resistant starches can also be difficult for some people to ferment, causing them problems with bloating, gas, discomfort and allergy-like symptoms.

For some people, the problem with complex carbohydrates doesn't stop there.

We know that simple carbohydrates are consumed by the truckload in modern society, contributing to diabetes, heart disease, intestinal diseases, obesity, mental problems and many others. However, complex carbohydrates are also responsible for a variety of health problems. In many people they contribute to digestive disorders, obesity, fatigue, depression and a host of other problems. And keep in mind that all starches - complex or simple - break down into simple sugars which contribute to blood sugar disorders such as weight gain and diabetes. Why, might you ask, is it that seemingly healthy whole grains such as oatmeal, wheat, rye and/or rice can be so unhealthy for so many people? It is probable that our evolution is to blame. The advent of agriculture so many centuries ago generated relatively new foods (i.e. grains) in an old food chain to which humans have apparently not physiologically adapted to. In fact, our ancestors were known to eat grains only in a fermented or sprouted form that increased their digestibility and preventing disease.

Furthermore, and interestingly enough, carbohydrates are not essential nutrients in humans: the body can obtain all of its energy from protein and fats. The body can synthesize glucose from protein and from triglycerides (a common storage form of fat produced by the body or supplied by food).

For these reasons, throughout this book there are frequent recommendations to eliminate wheat, glutens and/or all grains from many health-promoting diets. The proof is in the thousands of people who have regained their health by reducing or eliminating many or all of the grains from their diet.

STARCHES	SIMPLE SUGARS
• all grains (wheat, rice, barley, oats, rye, etc.) • potatoes - white, red, sweet, yams • corn • beans	• all fruit • milk

COMPLEX CARBOHYDRATES	REFINED CARBOHYDRATES
• oats • barley • buckwheat • potatoes • flourless breads • corn • peas • beans • lentils	• all sugar • all candy • chocolate • all baked goods • breads and crackers • processed cereals • pasta • jam • honey

Metabolic Syndrome - Insulin Resistance, Diabetes and Hypoglycemia

Metabolic syndrome includes any disorder than involves a blood sugar imbalance and is directly related to the over-consumption of sugars and starches, especially refined carbohydrates, and especially when combined with a lack of exercise. In fact, any foods with a high Glycemic Index that are eaten in excess increase the risk for metabolic problems. Insulin Resistance is the direct result of a high sugar diet that overtaxes the hormone system. Dietary sugars enter into the blood via the small intestine. Simple sugars that are derived from low fibre, high sugar foods and flours are very quickly absorbed, causing a rapid increase of blood sugar. The rate at which the sugar enters into the blood is known as the Glycemic Index. (This rapid absorption of sugar is also responsible for the "sugar highs" that affect behaviour and activity levels, especially as seen in children.)

Once sugar enters the bloodstream, it must find its way into liver and muscle cells, where it is either burned for immediate energy or is stored as glycogen for use later. In a healthy body, sugar is absorbed into the tissues with the help of insulin, a hormone produced by the pancreas. Insulin regulates blood sugar levels by attaching itself to specific receptors in the liver and muscles as well as in fat cells. Insulin then causes these receptors to open, allowing the passage of sugar from the blood into the tissues. Think of the receptors as gatekeepers that open and close and insulin as the key. In the presence of a long-term high sugar diet and sedentary lifestyle, how-

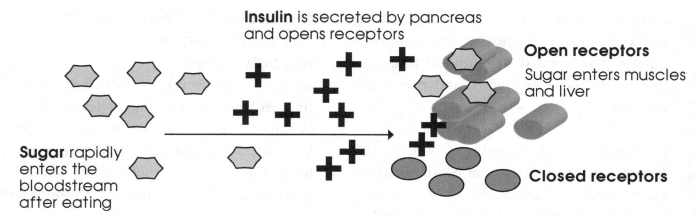

Insulin is secreted by pancreas and opens receptors

Open receptors
Sugar enters muscles and liver

Sugar rapidly enters the bloodstream after eating

Closed receptors

Insulin Resistance- ....high insulin levels but receptors no longer respond to insulin. Sugar must now convert to fat.

Figure 7

ever, these cell receptors become resistant to the effects of insulin and no longer open, as they block themselves off to protect the liver and muscle tissues from further damage by increasing sugar levels.

With nowhere else to go, these sugars are now converted immediately to fat instead of to glycogen, with the liver and new fat cells (i.e. weight gain) acting as storage houses for the excess fat. These storage depots are often recognizable as belly fat, a sign of a fatty liver. In the beginning, the blood sugar levels will actually test normal as the body produces higher insulin levels to keep the blood sugar under control. During the time that insulin levels remain high however, damage and inflammation to a number of body systems begins to occur, particularly to the liver, heart and cardiovascular system, eyes, kidneys and nerves. This is a significant occurrence because at any time that blood sugar levels rise, sugar levels in the tissues tend to drop, depriving extremities and organs of adequate levels of circulation and nutrients. This phase

can be considered as the pre-diabetic stage.

Over time, the insulin production eventually "wears out" as the pancreas exhausts itself and is no longer able to produce enough insulin to direct sugar to specific tissues. Now blood sugar begins to rise permanently. This condition of high blood glucose and insulin deficiency is known as diabetes mellitus, or Type II diabetes. It is the stage that often follows insulin resistance if the conditions of high dietary sugars and lack of exercise continue. There are hundreds of thousands of new cases of diabetes every year due to the increasing incidence of obesity, stress and sedentary lifestyles.

Insulin resistance is implicated in depression, anxiety, insomnia, attention deficit problems, hyperactivity and is a major factor in initiating the brain damage that leads to memory loss, cognitive decline, dementia and Alzheimer's. Some researchers are referring to Alzheimer's as "Type-3 Diabetes".

Symptoms of advanced metabolic syndrome can include blurred vision, fatigue, thirst, frequent urination, hunger, and weight loss (as the fat cells are burned for energy) with long-term implications for blindness, poor circulation, kidney failure, amputations from nerve damage, high blood pressure, strokes and heart attacks. Half of all reported cases of high blood pressure are caused by insulin resistance.

Once again, stress levels play a significant role in metabolic syndrome as the hormonal chaos it causes is particularly sensitive to stress levels. Stress elevates cortisol levels, a hormone produced by the adrenal glands. It acts as both an anti-stress hormone and as a natural anti-inflammatory against pain and inflammation. Normal cortisol levels help control carbohydrate metabolism and the metabolism of bone, muscle, nerves, heart, blood and intestines. Stress is nature's response to "fight or flight" situations and is nature's way of protecting us from danger by increasing blood pressure and breathing rate, tensing the muscles, maximizing vision and dumping extra sugar into the bloodstream for additional energy. However, in cases of chronic stress - when fight or flight is not possible - the continuing release of excess cortisol puts us at risk for a variety of different health problems but especially blood sugar disorders, since high cortisol levels increase insulin. Remember, high fat diets also increase insulin levels. Chronically high cortisol levels have several other effects, notably depression of immunity, muscle wasting, osteoporosis and weight gain.

Don't wait for medical tests to clinically confirm high insulin levels and/or blood sugar. If you're overweight, tired, sedentary, unfocussed and stressed out it's time to change your lifestyle – now!

Hypoglycemia is another word for low blood sugar caused by either high insulin levels or by high carbohydrate diets. While hypoglycemia can be a serious concern for insulin dependent diabetics who have administered themselves too much insulin, it is more often a sub-clinical condition whereby people frequently experience sweating, trembling, heart palpitations, hunger, and weakness. This type of low blood sugar is almost always caused by diet – namely refined carbohydrates, sugar, wheat flour, caffeine and alcohol. These foods cause a rapid increase in insulin followed by a crash in blood sugar.

In contrast to other organs, the brain depends on sugar almost exclusively. The brain cannot make its own glucose and is completely dependent on the body's provisions of sugar delivered by the blood. If blood sugar levels fall or if the brain's requirements increase and demands are not met, it results in mental symptoms such as confusion, poor concentration, poor memory, insomnia, fatigue, epilepsy, nervousness, irritability, anger and other mood swings. Show this to your partner if they're hard to live with and are addicted to sugar and caffeine.

The Importance of Fibre

Fibre is non-starch sugar that digestive enzymes are unable to break down. Different types of plants contain different forms of fibre, including cellulose, hemi-cellulose, lignins and pectins. There are two different types of fibre - soluble and non-soluble:

a) Soluble fibres dissolve in water and form a thick gel and are found in all fruits and vegetables, oats, and especially beans. The digestion of all nutrients takes place in the stomach and small intestine. It is here that the pancreas secretes a variety of different enzymes to digest proteins, fats and carbohydrates. Carbohydrates are digested into simple sugars. Soluble fibres slow down the conversion of starches (sugar, bread, grains) into sugars and the subsequent sugar absorption into the blood. The speed at which sugars from a particular food absorb into the bloodstream is known as the Glycemic Index of that food; soluble fibres lower the Glycemic Index and regulate blood sugar. Thus they have a direct influence on the prevention of diabetes and heart disease.

The formed gel from soluble fibres binds with bile acids secreted by the liver, aiding liver detoxification (bile drains toxins) as well as helping us to feel full longer and therefore preventing over-eating and obesity. And, since the digestive process is slower in the presence of fibre it allows more time for healthy nutrients to be extracted from food, increasing vitamin and mineral absorption. Soluble fibre slows down digestive transit time but doesn't increase fecal bulk as insoluble fibre does. However, soluble fibre ferments in the lower colon (after most of the food has been digested in the small intestine)

producing a number of short chain fatty acids which promote health and immunity. This is one of the reasons why it is so important to have adequate levels of probiotics in the colon: they ensure optimum digestion and immunity through the fermentation of fibre.

b) Insoluble fibre doesn't dissolve in water and comes from the cell walls of the stalky, woody parts of the plant. These include cellulose, hemi-cellulose and lignin and are found in whole grains (brown rice, bulgar, barley, wheat bran), flax seeds (lignins), beans (legumes), and coarser vegetables such as celery and carrots. Insoluble fibers bulk up the stool by binding to water, making stools softer and bulkier. This speeds up the passage of food through the colon, aiding the elimination of waste and lessening the colon's exposure to toxic substances produced during digestion.

High fibre foods are almost always low in fat, especially saturated fat. All fruit and vegetables contain both soluble and insoluble fiber, but depending on the type or maturity, the soluble to insoluble fiber ratio may vary. The removal of seeds, peels or hulls from any food always reduces fibre content.

Fibre Detoxifies the Body
All toxic chemicals all processed by the liver, whether they are environmental (pollutants, chemicals, food, alcohol and pharmaceuticals) or internal (toxic by-products from viruses, bacteria, yeast and fungi, metabolic waste products and colon toxins). Since most toxins are fat soluble, the liver must use a 2-step process to convert them into water-soluble substances for excretion. The first

step uses oxidation to make a toxic chemical more harmless. (This produces free radicals of course, thus the importance of using anti-oxidants for liver detoxification.) The second step contributes a sulphur based molecule to change the toxin from fat-soluble to water-soluble. The water-solubility allows the toxins to enter into the bile for excretion. This is why liver detoxification programs include sulphur based supplements such as glutathione, methionine or garlic.

Once the toxins are converted they are carried from the liver to the small intestine via the bile. Bile eliminates toxins and wastes as well as digesting fat. The soluble fibre in the small intestine binds with the toxic bile and carries it out of the body via the feces. A lack of dietary fibre results in the re-absorption of toxic and fatty bile back into the bloodstream and again into the liver, causing damage to the blood vessels, tissues and organs; and forming cancer-producing compounds.

No fibre; no health!

A lack of dietary fibre is directly linked to constipation, hemorrhoids, diverticulosis, many cancers including breast cancer and colon cancer, toxic liver diseases, cardiovascular disease, and diabetes.

I'm probably not your mother, but I think that you should eat your vegetables.

Protein - What Is It?

We use protein to build new tissues for growth, and to repair worn out or injured tissues. Protein is the main constituent of muscles, bone, cartilage, skin, hair and blood. Twenty percent of the bone matrix is also composed of protein. Most body functions require protein in many different forms. Adequate protein levels are also necessary for a healthy immune system as well as anti-oxidant activity. Protein consists of building blocks called amino acids. There are approximately twenty amino acids, twelve of which can be manufactured by the body. The other eight are "essential amino acids", meaning they must be provided through the diet. Dietary proteins are separated into amino acids in the small intestine and absorbed into the blood stream.

NON-ESSENTIAL AMINO ACIDS	ESSENTIAL AMINO ACIDS
• alanine	• arginine
• asparagine	• histidine
• aspartic acid	• isoleucine
• cysteine	• leucine
• cystine	• lysine
• glutamic acid	• methionine
• glutamine	• phenylalanine
• glycine	•threonine
• hydroxyproline	•tryptophan
• praline	• valine
• serine	
• tyrosine	

Can We Get Too Much Protein?

The harder our muscles work, the higher our requirement for proteins. Physical workers and athletes need more protein than those who live sedentary lifestyles. Muscle strength and muscle building requires more protein.

Protein (fish, meat and eggs) is digested in the stomach and small intestine. The digestion of all proteins should be complete before they reach the large colon. If protein is not fully digested before it reaches the colon, it will ferment there causing the production of unhealthy compounds. So, like any food group, excess dietary protein can be a problem when the input doesn't equal the output. Frequent high protein meals of steak and hamburgers for example, especially for the sedentary or the aged, results in this fermentation of proteins in the colon. During fermentation the bacterium in the colon then converts the protein (high in nitrogen) into ammonia. Like all colon toxins, ammonia is transported to the liver where it is converted through a number of chemical processes into less toxic urea, which is eliminated by the kidneys. However, once the kidney filters are saturated, ammonia begins to back up; excess ammonia is very toxic and will intoxicate the liver, preventing it from fully performing other important functions. This toxicity will also stress the kidneys and other major organs. If urea levels are consistently high, the kidneys will eventually become damaged, as the tiny filtration tubules begin to get clogged with excess urea.

Excess protein is also a factor in arthritic conditions. Much of the excess nitrogen that is not converted to urea will instead metabolize to uric acid, which is then deposited into joints and muscles, causing inflammation, soreness and, of course, gout. Acid conditions also affect bone density and strength, since the bones are often forced to give up calcium - which is alkaline - in order to buffer the acidic blood conditions. An acidic body condition always causes other health problems, due to increased toxicity in the liver and kidney. These problems include heart symptoms, artery damage, skin problems, glandular imbalances, joint and muscle pain, and fatigue.

Glycation - Sugar Coated Proteins

The structure of proteins determines their function, thus, when the shape or structure has been altered, the protein is unable to act normally. Sugar molecules are able to attach themselves to protein molecules (as well as to fat molecules) and permanently deteriorate the structure and function of the protein. These permanently disabled proteins are known as AGE's (advanced glycation end products); they are major players in the aging process. Their effects include cataracts, blindness, wrinkled skin, atherosclerosis (hardening of the arteries), weakening of the immune system, kidney failure, neuropathy and age-related brain disorders.

The average intake of added sugars in the typical North American diet is 15% of the daily diet or roughly 6-7 tablespoons per day! No wonder there is so much premature aging.

Protein for Weight Loss

When you eat any kind of food a certain number of calories are burned up simply by the energy required to digest, absorb, transport, utilize and store the food. This process is called thermogenesis. Of all the food groups, protein has the highest thermic effect, i.e. requires the most digestive energy for processing. Therefore, for every 100 calories of protein that you eat, you use up 30 calories just for digestion. Fats, by comparison, only use 2-3 percent of their total energy for digestion and contain twice as many calories per gram as proteins. No wonder you feel so engorged after a serving of French fries or cheese cake! Refined carbohydrates and sugars can have a thermic effect as low as 5-10 percent, with fibre and vegetables much higher. This is one of the major reasons why high protein diets work so well for weight loss: there is no excess energy for fat storage and there is an increased sense of satiety. Eating protein also stimulates the release of satiety hormones such as ghrelin or leptin, which regulate hunger and keep you feeling full longer.

Food Is Your Best Defense against Disease - Any Disease!

Vegetarians - Are They Healthy?

Let me first say that I wish I could be a successful vegetarian. Like so many of us, I dislike the thought of eating animal flesh and fish, don't particularly care for the taste and don't understand how anyone can kill an animal. Furthermore, the consumption of animal meat contributes, in a major way, to the environmental challenges of our precious land and water. And yet, if I had to rely on a long-term vegetarian diet I would be in very poor health…sad, but true. Unfortunately, this is most often the case with others; it seems that the nutritional requirements of our physical bodies are not yet in alignment with our philosophical beliefs and, for many of us, our spiritual evolution.

Over the years I have seen many very ill vegetarians suffering from impaired immunity, fatigue, muscle weakness, breakdown of connective tissue, colon and digestive diseases, skin disorders, edema (water retention), grey pallor, premature aging, and/or depression. Over the years, with my guidance, these determined vegetarians have tried many alternatives to eating meat: a balanced vegetarian diet; more nuts; more soy products; spirulina; vegetarian protein powders; combinations of rice, corn and beans and so on. I wish I could say that they were successful…but nearly every single one of them had to introduce meat protein back into the diet. I wish it wasn't so…

There are some ethnic groups however, which tolerate vegetarian diets more easily. Asians and East Indians for example, have a longer small intestine. Since it is from the small intestine that all nutrients – including proteins - are absorbed into the blood stream, a longer small intestine means that the body has more time to extract protein from grains. In contrast, those people of European ethnicity, which includes most Caucasians, have a shorter small intestine designed to digest meat very quickly.

Eat what your ancestors ate; and don't eat what they didn't.

It's all about balance. There are big meat eaters from any background who could really benefit from a vegetarian diet to heal their bodies of the ravages of excess flesh protein. And there are many vegetarians whose bodies are crying out for extra protein.

All I can conclude is that if you, as a vegetarian, are in optimum health you are in a wonderful place. But unfortunately, a number of vegetarians choose to be ill rather than eat meat. To them I say this: animals have an incredible capacity for unconditional service and sacrifice and think nothing of passing over the veil and leaving their bodies behind for you to use for sustenance. They are amazingly spiritually evolved and they do not, for a moment, want you to suffer. This is their job.

For those of us who must rely on flesh protein for good health – even if it's just a small amount – we are obligated to honour and deeply appreciate the millions of animals who sacrifice their lives every day to save ours. And, in return, we must fight for them to have a happy, healthy and high quality of life. These acts of caring and compassion raise the vibration of the entire globe for all species, especially the human one. Don't eat the vibration of suffering animals. And don't contribute to the suffering of animals.

And, on a similar topic, has it ever occurred to us that epidemic viruses such as mad cow, swine flu, bird flu, West Nile, etc. are perhaps contracted by animals in an effort to save the human species from themselves? These viruses have actually been created by humans through pollution, contamination, inappropriate feed, drug induced mutations, irresponsible breeding programs, genetic engineering and manipulation; humans are masters at unbalancing the natural order of biology. Is it possible then that the animals have harnessed these viruses in an effort to contain them in their own species to prevent illness and death to humans? And rather than recognizing the unconditional love and sacrifice behind the actions of these amazingly evolved beings, we simply absolve ourselves

of responsibility by blaming the animals - or even another human race - for propagating and perpetuating contagious diseases.

Buy Organic

The Case for Our Ancestors

There is archeological evidence that our ancestors in the Paleolithic period were lean, fit and free of heart disease, diabetes, obesity, cancer and other chronic illnesses. Their physical fitness was due to the hunting gathering life style, which demanded daily physical exertion to collect healthy food and water. The Paleolithic diet consisted of fruit, vegetables, nuts, lean meats, and polyunsaturated fats. No sugars, no refined grains, no concentrated oils, no trans-fatty acids, very little saturated fat, and no processed foods rife with additives.

The animals in the Paleolithic period were not fed corn, oats and grains, nor were they locked up in stressful confinement areas with no exercise. They ate plants and native grasses which were not yet modified to photosynthesize excessive starch to increase milk and meat production. Their meat was low in saturated fat and high in essential fatty acids.

As well, similar to all wild animal species, our Paleolithic ancestors did not over-eat at any one meal. They ate to satiety and quit eating. Chances are that, due to food shortages and supply, our ancestors lost weight in the winter time coming into spring lean and hungry and re-gaining body fat in the summer. Good thing: the practice of eating small meals is linked to longevity!

Considering the average North American diet, the condition of our food supply, and that most people are deficient in multiple nutrients, it is no surprise that the very foods that should sustain us are now poisoning us. Our hospital beds are full and our medical bills are through the roof because we eat modern food and live sedentary, yet stressful lives. And that, dear readers, is the number one cause of disease – period.

We all benefit from healthy balanced diets. We require low-fat, high fibre, whole grains (sometimes) and light proteins and as much organic, pesticide and chemical free food as is possible given each individual's circumstances. Eat "happy" food – happy plants and grains that haven't been smothered under toxic chemicals, or fish and animal proteins that have not been locked up in "concentration camps" and fed a daily diet of drugs before being slaughtered in high anxiety conditions. Wouldn't we better infuse ourselves with a radiant life force from plants and animals that are happy and raised with gratitude, honour and reverence? Take a moment every day to bless Mother Earth for providing us with our sustenance. We truly are what we eat!

Happy food makes Happy People

Emotional Relationships with Food

We can easily establish the link between diet and physical health but do many of us actually recognize the relationship of good food to emotional health. In fact, our relationship with food could very well be as important as our relationship with money or even people.

There are many similarities: food, money or people all cause us to experience a smorgasbord of emotions. They can cause us to act like someone other than ourselves, they can cause us to behave dishonestly, they can make us feel shamed, they can cause us to disregard the feelings of others…they can even cause us to hit rock bottom. If you can heal your relationship with food, I can guarantee that your relationships with both money and people will improve too. Or, if you prefer, you can heal your relationship with people or money first and watch your relationship with food change. It matters not where you choose to start, so long as you work toward being the best person you can be.

Don't let your dopamine levels control you; you can control your dopamine levels

Food – and drugs - routinely affect the brain, causing anxiety, depression, irritability and/or fatigue; food also has a profound effect on how we feel about ourselves. Excess weight, for example, not only affects physical health and self-esteem, but also acts as a storage depot for a variety of toxic emotions. When we lose weight, we release toxic emotions stored in the fat cells. Or, if we release toxic emotions first, we are then able to lose stubborn weight much more easily. This is why we can feel so disproportionately burdened down with heavy, unhealthy diets that trap us in a seemingly never-ending cycle: the more unhealthy food we eat, the more negative emotions become attached to it; the more negative emotions we accumulate, the more unhealthy food we will consume.

Body organs also store a variety of different emotions. For example, the heart can store disappointed love, the liver can hold anger, the stomach can experience fear, and the lungs can hold on to sadness. But in fact, there are no rules as to which emotions are stored in a particular location. Over the years, I have identified a lot of different emotions in people's organs and body systems and have found that there is a unique blueprint for everyone and it hardly ever fits a pattern. Food can accelerate both the storage and release of these different feelings which is why so many of us report huge spiritual shifts during different types of fasting and/or vision quests. Vital food allows for spiritual alignment, intuition and connection…

Feed the soul…

Here's how our psyche affects the foods we choose…

FOOD & MOOD

Sugar and candy - looking for sweet "pick-me-ups" or rewards;
low energy levels and depression

Cookies, cakes, pastries - needing reassurance, no sense of identity

Breads and pasta - needing comfort, calming or sedating; self-sympathy

Fat - filling the emptiness, feeling lost and hollow

Dairy Products - feeling anxious; nervous tension

Chocolate - needing love

Nuts - needing to have fun

Spices - looking for excitement or mental stimulation; low energy

Salt - fearing emotional pain; stress

Crunchy foods - feeling anger, irritability or aggression

Soft and creamy foods - having a passive nature, feeling defenseless

Ice - wanting to numb feelings; not wanting to deal with the situation

Liquids - up and down energy levels

Junk Food - lacking motivation; procrastination; inertia

Let's now take a look at specific foods and their effects on our immune system…

Chapter 2

FOOD ALLERGIES, INTOLERANCES and IMMUNITY
- Restore Your Health -

"What is food for one, is to others bitter poison"
.....Lucretius

The Power of Food Reactions

It's common knowledge that our food literally provides us with the staff of all life: vitamins; minerals; fats; proteins; and carbohydrates. It is these nutrients that give the human body structure, function and vitality. They keep our hearts beating, our muscles pumping, our blood running, our skin healthy, our lungs breathing, our energy high and our thought processes resembling sanity. What's not so common knowledge is how the food you eat can actually interfere with structure, function and vitality and not only create a variety of uncomfortable symptoms but also contribute to and actually cause a number of diseases. Just as healthy foods can help us restore health, unhealthy foods (which are often disguised as healthy ones) can keep us diseased and unwell. Eating healthy foods is beneficial and health-giving, but unfortunately, the damaging results of eating unhealthy ones over-power the goodness of wholesome foods. For example, you can eat salad greens, fruit and cruciferous vegetables several times per day, but if your habit of eating eight ounces of friendly bacteria-containing yoghurt with oats for breakfast every day is causing chronic sinus congestion, fatigue and/or nausea, your otherwise healthy food habits will never rescue you from your symptoms. Likewise, supplements and herbs will never be able to neutralize a food reaction; only the elimination of the offending food will give relief. A healthy diet, supplements and herbs can, however, be excellent therapies to prevent the immune system from deteriorating to the point of hypersensitivity in the first place.

What Are Food Allergies?

The word allergy is derived from two Greek words meaning "altered reaction". This altered reaction is an adverse immune response to a food protein (antigen), whereby the offending food invokes the release of antibodies to destroy it or to neutralize its action. The subsequent discharge of histamines and chemicals causes varying degrees of inflammation that can affect virtually any body system.

True allergy reactions most commonly cause symptoms of swelling or itching of the lips or tongue, skin hives, itching or rashes, difficulty breathing and/or diarrhea, nausea and cramping. Anaphylactic allergic reactions are life-threatening reactions that are often triggered by *nuts, fish, dairy products and eggs.* In other words, the violence of the reaction causes major inflammation, possibly resulting in closed airways, serious swellings and even loss of consciousness.

Food allergies, including anaphylactic shock reactions, indicate, not that there is a problem with the food, but rather that there is a problem with the immune system, an immune system that *can be healed.*

What Are Food Intolerances?

Food intolerances, on the other hand, are defined as sensitivity to certain foods caused by the body's inability to properly digest or fully process them, which leads to chronic symptoms and illness. Food intolerances or sensitivities mean that there is a problem with the food, most notably **dairy products, wheat products, sugar, and unhealthy, rancid fats.** The continued ingestion of these food groups over the years intoxicates and damages the colon through excess fermentation, causing an imbalanced colonic eco-system which not only predisposes it to colon diseases such as colitis or cancer, but also opens it up to the invasion of bacteria, viruses, yeast and parasites whose toxins damage the intestinal walls, making them more permeable. This abnormal permeability is known as "leaky gut" and allows the migration of all toxins and impurities into the rest of the body causing the auto-intoxication of any or all body systems, which result in a variety of toxic reactions.

Food intolerances can and do cause a variety of different symptoms in a variety of different body systems and can show no selectivity in their target, although it is apparent that food reactions are more likely to cause symptoms in those areas of the body that are already weakened or compromised. That's why different people exhibit such unique symptoms, even though they may be eating the same offending foods. Here are some common food intolerance "syndromes".

COMMON FOOD REACTIONS

Respiratory - coughing, asthma, congestion, bronchitis

Gastro-intestinal - diarrhea, constipation, bloating, nausea, cramping, ulcers, heartburn

Skin - hives, rashes, eczema, psoriasis, itching, acne

Urinary - bladder infections, frequent urination, bedwetting, cystitis, kidney inflammation

Immunity - susceptibility to viruses, bacteria, allergies, ear infections

Cardiovascular - atherosclerosis, heart arrythmia, blood pressure imbalances, circulation

Musculo-skeletal - arthritis, joint pain, osteoporosis, weakness, fibromyalgia

Neurological - headaches, vertigo, memory loss, tinnitus (ear ringing), fatigue

Brain - depression, anxiety, mood swings, ADHD and ADD, learning difficulties, mental dullness, inability to think, phobias, dementia

General - fatigue, hypoglycemia, starch and sugar cravings, diabetes, obesity

When Do Food Reactions Occur?

True allergy reactions are immediate and can occur within minutes or within two hours after eating. Relatively speaking, the faster they appear, the faster they disappear. Delayed food reactions are caused by food intolerances and can begin several hours later and very often will not appear until the following day with your first meal; *regardless of whether or not that first meal contains the hidden food allergen that caused the initial food reaction*. Subsequent meals not containing any allergens are also capable of renewing the reaction. It's as if the process of digestion causes another wave of antigen absorption and begins another antibody attack. In other words, you can eat a bowl of reactive oatmeal on a Tuesday and not have a reaction until Wednesday when you eat your first food whether it is a salad, a bowl of rice, or a piece of turkey. And furthermore, depending on the health of the immune system, the reaction can last anywhere from 12 to 72 hours. By this time, of course, you've likely eaten the offending food again, as well as others, and cannot understand why you feel so rotten every day. Delayed food reactions are almost always a result of hidden or unsuspected food sensitivities because they never give you an immediate reaction. The reactions are further complicated when more than one food or a food combination is causing symptoms simultaneously. This is what makes them so hard to identify. The good news is that the stronger the immune system becomes through good food and organ healing, the less time the reactions will last – a 3 day reaction will eventually reduce to 1 or 2 days, then to hours and minutes, and eventually no reaction at all.

Food reactions can be worsened by eating the offending food by itself on an empty stomach or by exercising immediately after eating - both increase the rate of absorption.

The amount of food required to cause a reaction can vary from amounts as small as one to two teaspoons to much larger portions.

Hidden food sensitivities cause people to suffer some of the most common, chronic and incapacitating of health problems. Unfortunately, they are not usually aware that foods have anything to do with their problems, so for years they keep buying symptom relief in the form of medication for years, without ever suspecting food problems; they have been convinced that their condition is incurable. *Of course, this is not true!* Read on…

The Allergy-Addiction Cycle

If a food has the power to be addictive I consider it a drug. It seems that we never become addicted to things that are healthy. When was the last time you couldn't get through the day without a carrot?…or found yourself obsessing over an avocado? ..or raiding the fridge at midnight for a piece of broiled fish? But time and time again, people will refuse to give up chocolate, coffee, candies, bread, sweets or potato chips. And, of course, their tobacco! These foods have all become destructive habits and people are now engaged in what is called the "allergy-addiction" cycle. The offending food is an absolute favorite: we love to eat it, it tastes great and the more damage and suffering that it causes, the more we crave it. These addictive foods are easy to identify; they are the ones we don't want to give up. We'd rather enjoy the "high" until, of course, we crash. Coffee is so energizing…until your nerves are shot. Fats are so filling…until you lose your gallbladder.

Tobacco feels so good…until you get cancer. You get the picture…

Like any addiction, the elimination of an addictive food can throw people into withdrawal symptoms. Very often the withdrawal symptoms mimic the symptoms that the food causes when ingested. Sugar addicts for example, after giving up sugar, will often describe feelings of fatigue, depression, poor concentration, irritability and mood swings. These symptoms are simply an over-exaggeration of the way they actually feel on sugar. But now the symptoms are intensified and the withdrawal brings to their attention that their normal state of being is anything but normal.

Why do we bother being addictive at all? Truly, this is the question of the ages, as addictions - food or otherwise - have been the bane of human society for centuries. What is apparent is an inherent destructive streak whereby we seek to do ourselves damage under the guise of an artificial "high". Carbohydrate addictions, similar to drug addictions, increase the levels of dopamine – a "feel good" chemical in the brain. All food addicts are "emotional eaters" and we use a variety of foods (and other harmful substances) to "beat ourselves up" and to *inflict upon ourselves what our perceived level of self-worth apparently deserves.* Oftentimes it seems easier to eat than to throw light on our shadows. Sadly, we have told ourselves so many lies and untruths about ourselves that we have succeeded in casting darkness over the true beauty of the inner light hidden within us all. As with other addictions, we commonly try to scare or shame people into good health or into losing weight by threatening them with death and disease. Save your breath – it's futile and it's cruel. Food addictions – like any other addictions – should be treated with compassionate and considerate care and supported with hypnotherapy, acupuncture, emotional freedom techniques, energy healings, homeopathy, flower essences and counseling - including relationship counseling - or any other therapy that "speaks" to you.

Seek Happiness …You Deserve It

What Causes Hypersensitive Immune Systems?

1) Lifestyle

The bottom line is that a body that is suffering from food allergies, intolerances and sensitivities has reached this state of ill health from self-inflicted lifestyle choices which have damaged the digestive system, leading first to colon toxicity, and then subsequently the immune system and other body systems. The continuous assault on the body by poor food choices, toxic diets, caffeine, smoking, alcoholism, prescription drugs, vaccinations, lack of exercise, and/or stress makes it very difficult for us to maintain anything resembling good health. Eventually the damage becomes extreme and the immune system collapses. The good news is that the damage can be reversed even though it may take some time, depending on the person's health history, how long they have been ill, and their level of sensitivity.

It does seem that people who are extremely sensitive to everything - the environment, people, emotions, energy fields and so on –

are also very sensitive to food. Makes sense, doesn't it? Don't fret about being sensitive: it's a blessing, not a curse. It allows one to achieve a deeper connection…to themselves, to others and to the world.

2) Toxic and Leaky Guts

All the food that we eat is digested in the mouth, stomach and small intestine. Carbohydrate digestion starts in the mouth by chewing, proteins are primarily digested in the stomach and the remaining proteins, carbohydrates and fats are digested in the small intestine where all the nutrients are absorbed into the blood stream. The waste products are then passed into the colon where water and electrolytes are reabsorbed after which the remaining waste is passed as stool. The problem begins with the ingestion of excessive carbohydrates, sugars and meats which strain the digestive capacity of the stomach and small intestine, which must then pass mal-digested food material into the large colon. The colon is not equipped to digest food; its job is to ferment waste material. Now it is forced to try and digest food through fermentation which produces numerous toxic by-products such as methane gas, heat, lactic acids and ammonia, plus more than twenty other chemical poisons. This cocktail of toxicity disrupts the natural balance of microflora by killing off beneficial bacteria and encouraging the over-growth of the unfriendly bacteria and yeast which produce more toxins and lactic acids. These poisons damage the intestinal lining of the colon making it abnormally permeable. This permeability allows the migration of bacteria, yeast, acids and toxins to leak across the membranes and into the general body systems, causing problems for the skin, liver, lungs, brain, nervous system, heart, joints, muscles and virtually any other system in the body. This internal toxicity has a major impact on the immune system too of course, causing it to malfunction and to react to a variety of food and environmental stressors.

3) Emotional Stress

The role of stress cannot be overlooked. Obvious stressors include job stress, marriage troubles, divorce, retirement, illness, death, studying for and writing exams, financial difficulties, relationship problems with friends, family or neighbours, abusive relationships, and even falling in love. Less obvious stressors that can nevertheless have a huge impact on immunity include deeply held sub-conscious fears that we may not even be aware of, such as hidden phobias.

Short or long-term stress affects our immunity by actually shrinking the thymus gland. The thymus gland is found below the forward base of the neck behind the breast bone and it produces billions of lymphocytes (antibodies) and immune hormones. During acute stress this gland shrinks to half its size within a day; millions of lymphocytes are destroyed and the immune system plummets. Now - without its normal defenses in place - the immune system will not tolerate even the slightest dietary indiscretions and our physical health deteriorates.

Periods of high emotional stress should always be supported with a healthy diet and the elimination of poorly tolerated foods, even though we are often drawn to doing the opposite by sinking ourselves further into a downward spiral by engaging in a junk-food fest. I've had clients over the years who were preparing to sell their businesses, get divorced, quit school, run away... all convinced that they could no longer cope and were suffering from an incurable emotional state from which there was no way out. It turned out that all that was required was an intelligent adjustment to their diet and nutrition. We humans really are interesting, aren't we?

Inhalant Allergies

When our physical and emotional vulnerability has compromised our immune system, inhalant allergies are likely to arise for the first time. Anytime the immune system is compromised by physical illness, such as colds and flus, the body can quickly acquire hypersensitivities to dust, pollens and molds. In these cases, people often think that they have a cold that has lasted for weeks or even months, when in actual fact they are now suffering congestion and ill health from their newly acquired inhalant allergies. Inhalant allergies are perpetuated through inappropriate diets – see Chapter 6.

No Food Reactions?

And what about those people who seem to be able to shovel anything down and never seem to have a food reaction? Not to worry, they have just as many food problems as the rest of us. Food problems are not always experienced as allergens or intolerances. In fact, the silent repercussions of a toxic diet, a leaky gut or the long-term effects of lectins (see below) for example are often much more insidious. Not only do clinical results in natural health practices validate this but study after study is exposing the links between diet and major diseases such as heart disease, high blood pressure, cancer, diabetes, arthritis, mental illness, migraine headaches, etc. etc.

Common Food Problems – Repeat Offenders

Offensive food culprits in a food sensitive person are most often those foods that are eaten regularly and repetitively. In fact, most food sensitivities are used as North American food staples – the more often you eat the food, the more likely you are to react to it. It is important to note that ANY food or food substance can act as a trigger for any kind of food sensitivity reaction. And ANY symptom is possible with ANY food reaction. I have named some of the most common repeat offenders here that, in my years of clinical practice, have seemed to cause the most problems for the most people.

The best motivator for eating well is feeling well.

Most Common Food Intolerances

Dairy Products

 This includes milk, cheese, sour cream, ice cream and yes, yoghurt. Small amounts of butter are usually tolerated since it contains very little allergy-causing milk sugar or protein.

Look for mucus congestion, asthma, ear infections, skin problems, joint pain, mood swings (especially children), fatigue and hormonal problems, including PMS and menopause. Of course, dairy is commonly associated with the obvious gastrointestinal problems of bloating, constipation, irritable bowel, colitis, gas and/or diarrhea.

Dairy is more harmful in pasteurized, processed milk because of the reduction of antibodies that bind to toxic lectins (see below).

Dairy products are an entirely different product today from what our grandmother's cow used to provide. Modern diets for cows, combined with drugs and lack of exercise, followed by the processing methods of pasteurization, homogenization, and fortification make it very difficult for our bodies to digest, assimilate, or even recognize that this is a real food. Thus, the stomach, pancreas and liver identify and reject this food group as a foreign invader. Furthermore, a balanced diet does not require dairy products for calcium intake. Calcium is readily available from many other foods that are low-fat, non-acidic, unprocessed and uncontaminated: green leafy vegetables, legumes (beans), sesame seeds, flax seeds, organic soy products, kelp, salmon, broccoli, almonds, dried fruit and oranges. Bear in mind though that many children often don't or won't eat a variety of different foods. It may be necessary therefore to supplement them with extra calcium.

Be sure to avoid calcium antagonists: those substances that deplete calcium levels and encourage bone loss. If you eat lots of beef, drink caffeine (coffee, tea, coca cola, chocolate) or phosphorus-containing soda drinks such as pop you will need to increase your calcium intake. Don't try to bypass a dairy intolerance by drinking milk that has digestive enzymes in it to break down lactose (milk sugar). It's just another way of forcing down the poison.

Wheat Products

Wheat is found in bread, crackers, bagels, cookies and pasta. Sprouted wheat products - such as flourless bread - are an improvement, but should still be avoided in the beginning of a new food program. Wheat is also a problem because of its high gluten content. Of all the gluten-containing grains wheat has the highest level, presumably making it the most allergenic. As humanity evolved glutens were the last to be introduced in our prehistoric diets and we have therefore had less time to learn to digest and assimilate them properly. Despite the fact that spelt and kamut are older forms of wheat that do not contain as much gluten, they are still problematic for the majority of wheat-sensitive people. Avoid them all. Look for common wheat reactions such as inhalant allergies, depression, ADD, phobias, chronic fatigue, headaches, constipation, diarrhea, irritable bowel, colitis, bloating, gas, heartburn, ulcers, hypoglycemia (low blood sugar), diabetes (high blood sugar), thyroid conditions, carbohydrate cravings and obesity, as well as yeast-type symptoms, both internal and external. Some people report feeling fatigued on a wheat-free diet. This is usually

because their iron levels have dropped. A liquid iron tonic alleviates this problem within a few days.

Sugar

Sugar is also labeled as sucrose, glucose, fructose, corn syrup, barley malt, dextrose, cane sugar, maltose, lactose, maltodextrin, sorbitol, mono-saccharides, polysaccharides, honey, molasses and brown sugar, to name but a few. High fructose corn syrup, found in many processed foods, is a chemical sweetener that actually increases appetite, causes blood sugar problems and is highly addictive. Sugar can be hidden in numerous foods since it is used as a common preservative and taste enhancer. Unhealthy sugar intake can cause colon toxicity, yeast conditions, insulin resistance, carbohydrate cravings, anxiety, hyperactivity, mood swings, depression, irritability, poor concentration, adrenal burn-out and fatigue and arthritis. Highly sensitive people will also have a problem with fruit – this is normally temporary. In addition, sugar is considered an anti-nutrient: it robs the body of nutrients required for sugar metabolism, depleting the body's reserves of chromium, magnesium, manganese, zinc and B-vitamins. Sugar addicts often like to combine it with caffeine for the added adrenaline rush. The average North American consumes a half of pound of sugar every day.

Avoid all artificial sweeteners: aspartame, acesulfame potassium, and saccharin, as these have all been linked to numerous health problems, including mood swings, migraines and cancer.

Caffeine

Caffeine is found in coffee, tea, chocolate, colas, and energy drinks. Caffeine is an alkaloid-containing psycho-active stimulant and a socially accepted highly addictive drug with a number of side effects and intense withdrawal symptoms. Common symptoms of caffeine toxicity are insomnia, irritability, increased stress levels, chronic bladder and kidney infections, frequent urination, prostate and testicle conditions, impotency, infertility, heartburn, heart arrhythmia, high blood pressure, headaches, bone loss, anxiety, restlessness, poor memory, liver toxicity, and hormonal imbalances, including menstrual irregularities, PMS and menopause.

Caffeine increases energy by increasing adrenaline and raising blood sugar levels which then causes an exaggerated insulin response producing a "letdown". This "letdown" triggers the yo-yo syndrome and people find themselves needing one caffeinated drink after another to eventually maintain not higher energy levels but normal or often sub-par energy levels.

Caffeine will also deplete minerals, especially calcium and iron. Depending on the level of sensitivity and/or the number of years a person has been drinking it, caffeine can become a health problem on as little as one cup per day. There is no safe level of caffeine consumption for some people.

Potatoes

Regular potatoes are a member of the nightshade family. They contain solanine (a toxic alkaloid) and phosphoric acid. As discussed in Chapter One, acids are linked to many unhealthy symptoms. Potatoes are a common culprit in rheumatoid arthritis, osteoarthritis, generalized joint and muscle pains, headaches and sometimes anxiety. It is the strongest food in the nightshade family, which includes potatoes, tomatoes, eggplant, and peppers. However, once potatoes have been eliminated the other nightshades often seem to be well tolerated. Sweet potatoes and yams are not in the same family and do not cause similar reactions.

Beef

When beef is eaten in excess it causes an accumulation of arachidonic acid (AA). AA is a fatty acid which converts into Omega 6 type prostaglandins (see Fats and Oils below) that are capable of causing inflammation leading to arthritis, joint pain of all kinds and muscle pain, as well as heart and artery diseases. If you are suffering from any of these conditions eliminate beef, potatoes and sugar…and increase your dietary fibre! In other words get off the "meat and potato" diet. It's just not good for your health. (Did you know that many of the pharmaceutical anti-inflammatory medications work by blocking the conversion of AA into inflammatory prostaglandins? Is it not more sensible to change your diet?)

Soy

The main problem with soy is that it is a trypsin inhibitor, an enzyme responsible for digesting proteins. Since soy products are 40% protein, these inhibitory properties can cause gas, bloating and indigestion. Soy also contains phytic acid which blocks mineral absorption, as well as phyto-estrogens which can be a problem for people with high estrogen levels. Some people can have a true allergic reaction to soy but very few are actually anaphylactic. If soy is tolerated, use it in moderation and preferably in its fermented form since this optimizes digestion. Fermented soy products include tofu, tempeh, miso and soy sauce. Always choose organic soy products; most non-organic soy products are genetically modified.

Eggs

A common allergen for adults and children, eggs are often responsible for stomach upsets with nausea or vomiting, eczema, hives, asthma and congestion. Egg sensitivities can be caused or aggravated by low iron levels/anemia.

Nuts

Nuts are a highly allergenic food group which can cause many symptoms, even if a person is not anaphylactic. Nut sensitivities can cause nausea, vomiting, asthma, hives, joint pain and heart palpitations.

Citrus Fruit

Citrus is more often a problem than other fruits because of the citric and ascorbic acids they contain. Citrus sensitive people experience arthritis, joint pain, muscle pain, eczema, indigestion, congestion and/or asthma. Essential fatty acid deficiencies can exacerbate citrus reactions.

Fats and Oils

A serious dietary problem (see Chapter 4): the ingestion of any kind of fat can cause digestive problems, fatigue, head pressure, and degenerative problems leading to chronic disease. Aside from the direct health effects of the oils themselves, the ingestion of either excess or unhealthy dietary oils causes a disruption of normal digestion. Fat actually wraps itself around other foods coating them with a film of grease; this creates a barrier that digestive enzymes cannot penetrate. This now causes a problem with mal-digestion. For this reason, fats and oils are major players in food allergies and reactions, despite the fact that there may not be immediate reactions to the fats themselves. The intolerance to fats is often complicated by a sulphur deficiency because the liver requires adequate levels of sulphur to decongest fats and oils. However, I might add that a sulphur deficiency is likely caused by the dietary excess of fats and oils in the first place? Like most food problems, it can be a repeating cycle.

Others

Be sure to test for glutens (rye, oats, barley), rice, chicken, tomatoes and drinking water, even though these are less often repeat offenders.

Lectins

Lectins are food proteins that have the ability to bind to membranes found in the arteries, organs, glands and intestinal walls. Once they do so they damage the cells, disrupt membrane function and initiate a cascade of immune and auto-immune reactions which eventually kill the cell. When this occurs in the colon, lectins participate in the "leaky gut" process, which, of course, contributes to the auto-intoxication of the entire body by allowing not only the existing colon debris to cross over into general circulation, but the lectins themselves to cross over as well. The lectins then bind to the surface of arteries, organs and glands - including the thyroid, pituitary, pancreas, kidneys, liver, brain, adrenals, ovaries and testicles. The subsequent inflammation and cell damage leads to food reactions, hormone imbalances, auto-immune disorders and degenerative diseases.

Since lectins can cause such toxic reactions it is no surprise that they are found in large amounts in the following common problem foods already discussed above. We seem to be following another food "pattern"…hmmm…

Foods High in Lectins

Grains: Lectins are high in gluten-containing grains - wheat, wheat germ, oats, rye, and barley. They are also present in millet, rice, quinoa and buckwheat. Wild rice and white rice do not contain lectins. The grain-lectin relationship is a definite factor in colitis, celiac and Crohn's.

Dairy products (all): All dairy products are a lectin problem, especially now that commercial dairy cows are fed grain instead of grass. Dairy lectins have even been implicated in juvenile diabetes.

Nightshades: Potatoes (in particular), tomatoes, peppers and eggplant are all high in lectins.

Certain nuts, seeds and legumes: Peanuts, soy beans, nut and seed oils (peanut, canola, sunflower and soy) are also high in lectins.

Eggs: Eggs are high in lectins.

GM (genetically modified) foods are modified by splicing lectins from one plant family to another. This means that a particular food with which you have had no history of problems could now be toxic to you. How confusing…

Lectins are strong proteins that seem to be resistant to stomach acid and digestive enzymes. We therefore don't have the inability to deactivate or prevent them from binding to target tissues and organs. Unlike food allergies, lectins are toxins that invoke immune responses by causing damage to tissues through antibody attacks, leading to inflammation, auto-immunity and degeneration. (Food allergies, on the other hand, provoke an antibody immune response.) Hypersensitivity to lectins is likely a result of the modification of original food groups, poor dietary health, and the frequency of ingestion since these foods are often eaten as dietary staples. Lectins cause the same potential health problems as the food intolerances listed above.

And so it stands that the current North American diet containing staples of wheat, glutens, dairy products and potatoes are filling up our hospitals and draining our medical bank account.

Oxalic Acids

Oxalic acid is a strong, toxic and corrosive acid that is naturally occurring in some plants. It is 3,000 times stronger than vinegar (acetic acid) and in concentrated form is used in industry as bleach and as a disinfectant. Luckily the oxalic acid in plants is diluted. However, certain people have sensitivity to these acids resulting in a variety of symptoms. Oxalic acid binds with calcium in the digestive tract preventing excess absorption. There is also evidence that diets high in long chain fatty acids, such as some animal and fish fats, increase the absorption of oxalates from the colon. So now, not only do dietary fats slime your protein and your carbohydrates, interfering with their digestion, they also increase the unhealthy absorption of these acids. Once again – no surprise - high fat diets are implicated in digestive disorders leading to adverse health effects.

In a healthy colon oxalates are metabolized by probiotics (friendly bacteria) or eliminated in the feces. Oxalic acid can also be excreted in the urine by combining with calcium or magnesium to form salt oxalate. Excess oxalic acid can therefore deplete calcium and magnesium levels, in which case it cannot stay in solution and ends up crystallizing in various body tissues, causing damage there. The crystals of oxalates are small and very sharp causing pain and irritation to these tissues. Excess oxalates are implicated in rheumatoid arthritis, osteoarthritis, joint pain, kidney disorders (including stones which are composed of calcium oxalate), bladder irritations, gout, fibromyalgia, fatigue and an increase of general food allergies.

High oxalic acid foods:
Rhubarb, spinach, strawberries, citrus peel, coffee, chocolate, wheat, nuts, beets, black tea, draft or canned beer.

Other oxalic acid foods:
Blackberries, blueberries, raspberries, figs, papayas, kiwis, oranges, tomatoes, peppers, artichokes, kale, celery, olives, parsley, green beans, ginger, sweet potatoes, beans, tofu.

People with oxalic acid sensitivities should supplement with magnesium, calcium, potassium and probiotics. Lemon juice will increase the excretion of oxalates.

People keep buying symptom relief in the form of medication for years without ever suspecting food problems; they have been convinced that their condition is incurable.

The Seven Step Treatment Program for Food Allergies, Intolerances and Reactions

1) Elimination of Offending Foods

The first step in any kind of food reaction is elimination of the offending food. It is here that kinesiology is an outstanding tool to identify the foods or food groups that are causing the symptoms. Depending on the condition of the body - including the immune system - as well as the health of the gastrointestinal system, these foods may have to be eliminated for several weeks or months. It is important that the immune system has sufficient time to "clear" the allergic response and heal from the bombardment of a long-term assault. It is not necessary to eliminate twenty or thirty foods, as is often recommended by other methods of detection. The goal is to eliminate the *primary food* culprits while simultaneously *detoxifying the body, replenishing deficiencies and healing the immune system.* At this point, most secondary food reactions will simply dissolve.

See Kinesiology chapters for testing methods.

2) Elimination of Fats and Oils

Eliminate all oil extracts and foods containing added oils. As discussed in *Fats and Oils*, oils are an underlying cause of food reactions that significantly diminish digestive function. You may, however, use foods that are rich in natural oils such as avocado, salmon, olives or seeds.

3) Colon Cleansing and Detoxification

The connection between a congested, toxic colon and food reactions is significant. The presence of mal-digested food material, mu-cus, bacteria, yeast and acids ultimately damages the colon membranes causing "leaky gut". The resulting auto-intoxication damages the immune system, making it hypersensitive. The more acidic the colon, the more food reactions will prevail. A body that is in a healthy state of alkalinity has fewer problems with allergies of all kinds. An acidic, leaky gut is capable of causing a myriad of health problems including poor immunity, skin problems, headaches, asthma, digestive problems, muscle and joint pain, arthritis, depression and/or anxiety.

Bear in mind that colon toxins are detoxified by the liver, thus a toxic colon is synonymous with a toxic liver. Too often, the focus is on liver cleansing without detoxifying the colon. Don't put the cart before the horse – either cleanse the colon first or cleanse both organs simultaneously.

The most efficient gastrointestinal cleansing diet for many people is to eliminate ALL grains and eat only fruits, vegetables and a small amount of animal-based protein, with an emphasis on seafood and poultry.

If your system shows signs of dehydration or high acidity as indicated by joint pain, body pain, sinus problems and/or multiple food allergies consider drinking alkaline water. Acidic body systems are implicated in many diseases including, of course, an over-reactive immune system. Alkaline water encourages the pancreas to produce bicarbonate ions, resulting in an alkaline digestive system. Find a water depot that sells it, rather than using alkalizing "drops". See

Chapter 6 for colon cleansing supplement programs and Chapter 7 for testing diet programs.

4) Identify Dysfunctional Organs

Organ function is critical to our entire well-being. Our organs are not pieces of machinery that can go on indefinitely without due care and attention. They have a life span and they need love and proper nutrition to do the best job that they can. All of the body's organs contribute to immunity and to metabolism, however it is the colon, liver, pancreas, small intestine and stomach that has a direct relationship to digestion; and it is the thyroid, thymus and adrenals that have a direct relationship between food and immunity.

See Kinesiology chapters for testing methods and organ remedies.

5) Identify Nutrient Deficiencies

Customize a supplement therapy program by identifying any nutrient deficiencies, including vitamins, minerals, essential fatty acids, anti-oxidants and nutriceuticals. Nutrient deficiencies are major contributors to the presence of food reactions, including anaphylaxis. Nutrients play a very important role in the digestion, absorption and metabolism of all foods. Metabolism refers to how the body processes energy. Metabolic pathways are mediated by enzymes which depend entirely on vitamins and minerals for their action. Lacking even one nutrient can block these pathways, leading to digestive malfunction, organ toxicity, immune dysfunction and ultimately food reactions. For each individual, there is a critical amount of each nutrient that is required for normal and healthy function.

See Kinesiology chapters for testing methods.

6) Homeopathy

Homeopathic remedies can be very helpful for both chronic and acute food reactions. Remedies for chronic cases should be discussed with an experienced homeopath; however here are some useful recommendations:

Arnica – helps with any kind of acute inflammation – all food reactions cause some level of inflammation. Use up to a 1m potency depending on the intensity of the reaction.

Nux-Vomica – helps to detoxify the liver and clear irritating food reactions. Also very helpful for withdrawal symptoms from sugar, carbs and/or caffeine. Use a 30c daily for at least 14 days.

Thymuline – use to build up the immune system. Use a 30c or 200c daily for 2-3 weeks.

Apis – use for any reactions which involve swellings. Use a 200c every 4 hours, as needed.

Arnica, Thymuline, Adrenalinum – use this combination in a 30c or 200c as a homeopathic anti-histamine for acute food reactions. (It may also be used for inhalant and environmental allergies).

7) Identify All Stressors, Acute and Chronic

Realize that both conscious *and* sub-conscious stress, fear, anxiety, phobias and worry markedly reduce thymus function. This seriously compromises the immune system, leading to hypersensitivity and multiple allergies. Even becoming newly aware of our hidden stressors will begin to help.

See Chapter 6 for testing emotions.

For How Long Should Food Problems Be Avoided?

Once the body has reached a certain level of health and the immune system has had time to recover and rebalance, some foods can be re-introduced in moderation, without a negative effect. Sometimes they won't be tolerated if eaten daily but can be tolerated if eaten no more than once every four days. Everyone is different and some foods will cause a reaction every time they are eaten. However, the North American staple foods - wheat, dairy products, beef, coffee, sugar, and poor quality fats - that have clearly got us into trouble in the first place should be kept to a minimum. They are toxic and disease-causing and should not be eaten on a regular basis at any time.

What Next?

Now that we have laid a strong foundation of knowledge - food groups, food intolerances, and the power that food has over our physical, emotional and spiritual well-being - we need to find a way of determining the individual and very unique requirements that each of us has during any given time in a health situation. Meet kinesiology...

Chapter 3

THE ART OF KINESIOLOGY
- Energy Testing -

What is Kinesiology?

Kinesiology is a type of muscle testing used to evaluate health status. It can also be used to ascertain specific health, diet and nutrition requirements. It involves testing the body's response by applying pressure to a muscle - usually an arm muscle - to assess strength. The muscle will become stronger, weaker or remain neutral when certain foods, nutrients or other substances are placed within the energy field. The muscle will also respond when specific body organs, energy points and meridians are energetically addressed. I therefore prefer to refer to it is as *energy testing* since the muscle itself is simply used as an instrument to assess body function and status.

(Energy testing differs from *applied kinesiology* which is a technique that involves testing the strength of a variety of different muscles to determine the level of communication between those specific muscles and the brain. Imbalances are often corrected by massaging acupressure points. This method of kinesiology is popular with chiropractors and other related body workers.)

Energy testing is made possible by the understanding that anatomical body parts and systems including connective tissue, blood, the nervous system, the immune system, and all body organs are surrounded by an electromagnetic field. This field is a fundamental force of nature. It is a *physical* field that is produced by electrically charged particles and is a combination of an electric field and a magnetic field. The interaction between these two fields is mediated by units of light: these photons and the fields themselves are subject to a number of variables that can and do induce change.

Each body system, including the whole body, has a very unique field with different frequencies, wavelengths and colours, resulting in a "pattern". Each field is so unique that it can be considered a "fingerprint", in that no two energy fields look alike. Not only is each body system and organ surrounded by an energy field, but the particles and photons of which those parts are composed each vibrate at their own specific frequency. In fact, this is what creates all matter: the vibration and frequency of billions of energy fields. The frequency of vibration determines the identity of the substance and its shape, form, mass and colour. That's right – all matter, whether it is a physical body, a tree, a rock, a tomato, a table or a telephone is nothing more than a group of vibrating particles held together by light and intention. *Putting intention on anything means to feed it with information.* This is the foundation of knowledge necessary for all energy healing: that if matter is nothing more than light and intention then all matter is totally within our power to change.

This energy field, when seen as a whole around a living organism (or an inanimate object for that matter), is commonly known as the aura. An aura surrounds every living thing, including all body systems and organs.

In other words, not only does the physical body have a soul, so does each of its parts. This is why you should be kind to your liver, your heart, your brain and whatever other body part you may value. Auras differ in color, intensity, size and shape and when all the systems are functioning as they should be there is an orderly harmonious flow of energy. When physical, mental or emotional health problems develop, the energy fields become impeded and blocked, losing its harmonious flow, resulting in chaos and a break in intercellular communications. Interestingly enough, similar disease states have similar "energetic signatures". Experienced medical intuitives recognize these similar vibrations and are often able to identify problems based on the "pattern". And furthermore, within the aura lies an energetic blueprint of past, present and future traumas, illnesses, diseases and sometimes destinies. Bearing in mind that these events are nothing more than energetic patterns, healing is possible at all levels. This means that it is actually within our power to let go of the past and to alter the course of the future by changing the present.

...if matter is nothing more than light and intention then all matter is totally within our power to change.

Why Use Kinesiology?

Energy testing opens up a pathway of communication between all of these energy fields and the conscious awareness. It also allows us to enter the collective consciousness wherein lies an infinite amount of information, all of which can contribute to recovery. It has an amazing potential to give us profound information, allowing us insight into the fascinating world of energy medicine and teaching us new things every time we practice. When combined with a solid foundation of knowledge it is a powerful and specialized healing discipline.

Kinesiology enables the healer to "read" or "track" the body and many of its functions. It enables us to identify energy fields that are blocked or dysfunctional, to identify the underlying cause and to then assess what is necessary to correct the imbalance. Underlying causes can include nutrient deficiencies and excesses, dietary indiscretions, toxins, organ breakdown, injuries, shock, emotions, trauma, belief systems, influences from others and spiritual experiences.

Kinesiology is often capable of detecting problem areas long before they are found with conventional medical tests. That is because all imbalances first manifest themselves in the energy or vibratory field before they manifest as a physical problem, whether internal or external.

Kinesiology is safe, non-invasive, comfortable and relaxing. And – unlike various computerized versions - allows the tester to use their intuition or "feel". Kinesiology can be used by those who consider themselves non-intuitive. However, as we will learn in this book, the two skills are very much the same and intuition often begins with or develops from the practice of energy testing itself.

The practical benefit of kinesiology is that it can be performed frequently without being labour or cost intensive. This is important for testing diets and foods since problem foods can change quite rapidly even from week to week – especially for those people with allergic constitutions.

The body of a living organism is an extremely complex system that is governed by thousands of actions, interactions, and external variables. It is virtually impossible to make sense of this complexity, especially when it malfunctions, without using some method to "track" the various energy fields. We need to learn to screen out what is unimportant to the issue at hand. Instead, perceive the imbalances as part of a much larger whole whose parts can create chaos virtually anywhere within the system: the domino effect. These parts, and therefore the whole, can be put back into balance by tracking the imbalance back to its source and then restoring the original flow of the energy fields, either through physical modalities such as nutrition, herbs, homeopathy, and bodywork or through a variety of different energy healing therapies, including visualization, healing hands, prayer, psychic surgeries or qi gong, for example.

Amazingly enough, very often the only therapy that is required is for the healer to observe the cause of distress at the energetic level, at which point the energy field restores itself back to balance. This change in energy - as precipitated by the act of observation - is a quantum reality: once observed, the dysfunctional energy field collapses and transforms into a healed state. These types of spontaneous healing - often referred to as "miracles" - are accomplished through genuine compassion and the ability to enter into that dimension where light and information are pliable. The same is true of all energy healings.

Kinesiology removes the guesswork and gives the practitioner a solid tool within a practical framework to make sense of the situation and to share this interaction with the client. The client can not only feel the difference themselves in muscle strength but can also often immediately feel the energy shifts as created by the practitioner's intention to heal. In fact, it is such a subtle yet powerful system of healing that very often my patients wake up feeling better the morning of their appointment before we even meet. Their energy fields are already shifting in anticipation of the session! The power of these incredibly sensitive energy fields cannot be underestimated. Practically

anything is possible, the only obstacle being our own belief systems.

Do less and heal more.

Kinesiology also has exceptional value in working with those who do not verbally communicate with ease: the very young; the very old; the very ill and our beloved animals of all species.

How Does Kinesiology Work?

When testing specific supplements, kinesiology works by checking the resonance of a particular substance, remedy, vitamin or food against the resonance of the body's electrical field. Remember that all substances have a unique vibration. When the two electrical fields are disharmonic or dissonant, the muscle being tested will feel weaker. When the resonance is neutral, the muscle strength won't change. When the resonance is harmonic, indicating benefit, the muscle will feel stronger and have more resistance.

When testing specific body functions, organ points and/or meridians, a weakness, blockage or sensitivity will show up as a weak muscle test. As soon as we put our focus on an area of imbalance the disturbed flow of energy will create an immediate response throughout the entire system, including the testing muscle. At this point we are in direct communication with the client's energy field.

Think of standing beside a stranger in a line-up – sometimes you find yourself stepping back a few paces to increase the distance between your two energy fields. With no conscious awareness, your aura is uncomfortable with the subliminal energetic interaction which causes you to take conscious action. Or conversely, you find yourself striking up a conversation with a stranger simply because it "feels" good and you want to keep talking forever. These are examples of dissonance and resonance. And, even though it seems inexplicable at the time, there are usually some very good reasons for these behaviours. And speaking of feel, "feel" is when you intuitively know what action to take to harmonize the interaction in any relationship, including those with people, animals, nature and your own body systems. It is this "feel" that allows for superior results in all of our relationships and energy healings alike.

Matter is just light and information that our intentions have the power to change.

The Importance of Knowledge

Advanced practitioners or those people who are studying kinesiology as a serious discipline should have an understanding of anatomy (body structure) as well as physiology (how the different body systems function). The more knowledge that you have, the more information the client's energy field can give you. You cannot expect to rebuild your car engine if you don't even know how to open the hood. Or build a new house without a hammer. It is also beneficial to have knowledge of the properties of remedies and supplements and of their actions upon the body. Not only will the knowledge give you more accurate results, but in time you will feel the vibration of the substance itself.

The information that is gleaned from a testing session is not to be considered as random bits and pieces. The inquiring mind will seek to view the "whole" picture by connecting the dots – the resulting image will be of the integrated whole, rather than its individual parts. It makes no sense to identify that a client has numerous vitamin and mineral deficiencies and then send them out the door loaded with several different bottles if we have no idea how they acquired such poor nutritional status. We need to first ascertain the cause: whether, for example, it is a result of poor diet, malabsorption, stress and/or addictions.

Use knowledge as your bank account and the technique of kinesiology as the debit card with which you withdraw information. Think of mastering a musical instrument: first you learn to read, count and listen, then after much skill and practice you finally weave together knowledge with the art of expression, resulting in music. In the same way, knowledge combined with the art of healing results in the exquisite harmony of good health.

Use knowledge as your bank account and kinesiology as the debit card with which you withdraw the information.

In fact, the type and degree of knowledge and intention held by the tester is a significant factor in the outcome of results. This is one reason why different practitioners can get different results – the flow of intention and interaction between practitioner and patient becomes another unique "fingerprint". A kinesiology-practicing chiropractor versus a nutritionist will undoubtedly formulate two entirely different programs for the same condition. Is one more correct than the other? No. While knowledge can be considered a science, the practice of kinesiology is an art, the accurate performance of which is very much determined by the knowledge base of the practitioner. While there is no universal truth in health care, success lies in the ability always to identify the underlying cause(s).

What Can Kinesiology Identify?

Energy testing can be used for anything from a simple test to determine whether or not a supplement or food is agreeing with you to more advanced testing to determine if the different functions of an organ are in harmony. Complete programs can be successfully formulated with all of the corrections necessary to restore health. This book will describe techniques that can be used by both the beginner and the advanced practitioner.

You'll never know everything but it helps to know a lot.

Kinesiology, in combination with intuition, is also a useful tool for accessing "censored" information hidden in the subconscious. This can be extremely powerful since anything that remains hidden from us can be thought of as a shadow. From a psychological perspective, shadows grow stronger and stronger until the subconscious can no longer contain them. It is at this point that they break through our consciousness, causing uncomfortable emotions such as grief, depression, anxiety,

anger, fatigue etc. The intensity of these emotions can range from minor discomfort to a full-blown nervous breakdown. However, if the shadow sees the light of our awareness before it builds to the bursting point, it weakens, and as we heal, eventually fades away.

Energy testing helps differentiate between a physical cause, an emotional cause, a mental cause and a spiritual cause. The first and most important task for the healer is to determine which "energetic body or bodies" is most troubled. Sometimes it's all emotional, sometimes it's all physical and sometimes it's a combination of any of the four bodies: physical, emotional, mental or spiritual.

Always keep an OPEN MIND and DON'T MAKE ASSUMPTIONS. For example, it cannot be assumed that someone's chronic headaches and depression are caused by their abusive past or that another person's back pain dates back to a car accident. You must go in and track the fields and open up the knowledge base. This will necessitate that you leave your own agenda outside the treatment room. This allows you to work from the clients' agenda only – horse, hound or human. Kinesiology is one of the simplest and most effective methods for identifying problems... but don't make assumptions! And never assume that because it happened to you it's happening to your client.

Don't let your own experiences slant your results.

What Can Kinesiology Not Identify?

Kinesiology cannot be used to medically diagnose disease. Attaching a label to a set of symptoms is a right-brained exercise known as a diagnosis and has no meaning within the energy field. The disturbed field seeks balance by restoring flow and harmony, not by trying to fit itself into an arbitrary set of rules. The right-brained and analytical viewpoint of allopathic medicine relies on a diagnosis to determine the correct medication prescription as taught during medical training. But since no health symptoms that I have ever worked with are caused by a deficiency of drugs, holistic practitioners should have no interest in obtaining a diagnosis.

Kinesiology cannot be relied upon to give you *yes* or *no* answers. This is very important. Asking yes or no questions are right-brained exercises which have no meaning to the subconscious. The subconscious receives, stores and transmits information in symbols, **not in words**. *Are you pregnant? Do you have cancer? Will I be traveling to Europe next year? Should I buy a new car? Is this an emotional problem? Should I get married? Are you ready to die?* These are examples of inappropriate questions that will confuse both the tester and the client and can NEVER be relied upon

for accuracy. As well, these issues are often extremely emotionally charged, therefore the questions will immediately "freak out" the energy field causing erratic spark-like energy that breaks the flow of communication.

No method of testing, including blood testing or computerized techniques, is 100% reliable. There is a variety of different reasons why false positives and false negatives can occur with any method. However, kinesiology, done by a competent and mindful practitioner, can offer some of the best results because it allows people the opportunity to benefit from the extraordinarily revealing combination of communication, knowledge and intuition.

 Kinesiology is one of the most valuable tools in the tool chest, helping to integrate individual parts into the whole, helping to solve and resolve perplexing health problems and medical mysteries, and providing a base from which we never stop learning. And most importantly, done with an open heart, kinesiology gives us a method to open the collective consciousness in order to connect with one another on a profound level – human to human...human to animal ...soul to soul...spirit to spirit.

Let's now move on to some techniques, and learn the most effective ways for communicating, extracting and sharing all this light and information we've been talking about.

Chapter 4

THE PRACTICE OF KINESIOLOGY
- Methods and Techniques -

Testing another Person

There are two basic body positions in which energy testing can be performed easily and effectively. When testing only a few things and the session is short, the muscle testing can be done while standing. For longer sessions, it is recommended that the subject be lying down to avoid tiring them out and also to ensure that you can focus and take the time to think things through. Don't rush a session and compromise the results. Let it take the time it takes...

Standing Position

Face your test subject directly and ask them to hold their arm out in front of them at a 45 degree angle. With one hand, apply a *small* amount of pressure to the upper hand or wrist with either the palm of your hand or your fingers. Using the palm of your hand will give you more force for stronger individuals. Always use the hand that is on the same side of your body as the hand you are testing. Don't cross your arm in front of your subject – this blocks the energy field.

Ask your subject to simply hold their arm in place with their regular strength. They should not push back or give in but just hold. This prevents them from either getting into an arm wrestle with you or becoming too weak. Don't have the subject hold their arm up at shoulder height –

in front or at the side. This is a tiring position that doesn't give a lot of sensitivity because they can offer too much resistance. It is not necessary to place your free hand on their shoulder: it is better to keep this hand free for touching testing points and meridians. It is important to face your subject directly rather than standing off to the side or behind them. Facing the subject directly puts you in a "warm" position to receive information-containing energy. Standing beside them or behind them is "cool" and not only blocks the energy flow but also emits an unconscious body message that you are detached and un-comfortable with getting close. You want to merge your energy field with the energy field of your subject – this connection is what en-ables you to receive valuable information.

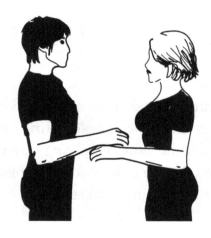

Subject Lying Down

Have the subject lying down on a comfort-able body work table and stand at their side, facing across their body. You can stand on either side; most people prefer to stand on the left hand side. Ask the subject to bend their elbow, resting it on the table beside them. Once again, simply ask them to hold their arm in position without either pushing

or going limp. Place your left hand against their outside left wrist/lower hand and push their arm down toward the table. Apply just enough pressure to be able to sense a differ-ence in strength.

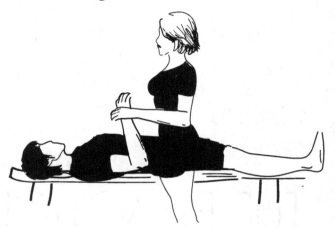

Surrogate Testing - Children and Animals

A surrogate is an intermediary – basically a conduit between the practitioner and the person or animal being tested. A surrogate is required when a person, child or an animal is unable to provide any muscle resistance to participate.

To use this technique, have the surrogate face you directly, with one of their arms avail-able for the resistance test and their free hand lightly touching the subject. All tests are per-formed with the intention on the subject, using the surrogate's muscle resistance to express the strengths and weaknesses of the subject.

Surrogate testing is a superior method of test-ing compared to self-testing. It's honest, ob-jective and the interaction between two peo-ple allows for a wonderful channel of healing energy to flow. This healing flow is possible because we are all connected via the network of omnipresent divine energy. All we have to do to activate this energy is to interact with each other for the higher good.

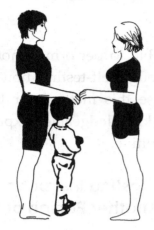

Remote Testing

You may also use surrogate testing to test people or animals who are not physically present, in which case it is best to work from a photograph. Using this method, you can actually lay food or supplements directly on the photograph, or, to test organ points or body systems, you can touch the corresponding points on the picture (see Chapter 6). This is an advanced technique that not only provides accurate results but also precipitates the same profound flow of healing energy.

Self-Testing

There is a variety of different ways to perform a self-test. However, it must be pointed out that achieving accurate results by self-testing can be very difficult…and especially so for beginners. The more attached you are to the outcome of the test the less likely you will be able to get accurate readings. If you test yourself on chocolate for example – your absolute favourite food that you can't get

through a day without - to determine if it is related to your headaches, your unwillingness to let it go will override any objective results. Likewise, if you are feeling desperate over relieving a health concern or a physical or emotional discomfort, your attachment to the outcome will be virtually impossible to break. In these cases it is best to see a practitioner or at least have a partner help you. Testing with another person always brings objectivity to the process, and helps to balance any strong emotions that you may be attaching to the outcome.

However, here are three methods of self-testing that can be useful if done correctly. Ensure that you are completely focused with your eyes closed and concentrating on the issue. Ideally, it is good to be in a semi-meditative state.

Finger Test

Press down on the knuckle closest to the fingernail on your forefinger, using the tip of the middle finger of the same hand. When testing foods or supplements hold the particular substance near your sternum while testing the forefinger strength – a weakened finger indicates negativity whereas a strong finger indicates a positive vibration.

Body Test While Standing

Stand up and keep the body in a relaxed position. Bend the knees very slightly and keep the feet parallel. With one hand, hold a particular substance close to the sternum, close your eyes and allow the body to either tip forward or backward. A backward tip indicates a weak or dissonant response while a tip forward indicates a strong or resonant response that the food or supplement is of benefit. This position lends itself well to a blind test of foods or supplements where you don't know what you are holding, thereby increasing the accuracy. Put the different foods or remedies inside similar containers such as small jars or baggies, hold them up against your sternum without looking and then set them down in two groups – negative and positive. If you have a lot of them, you can re-test everything in the "positive" group to narrow down what you are taking to only those foods or supplements that are of the most benefit.

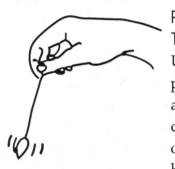

Pendulum Testing

Use any kind of pendulum, usually a crystal or copper at the end of a string, and hold the pendulum over the substance that you wish to test. Keep your fingers flexible enough to allow the pendulum to move, and keep the pendulum at least eighteen to twenty-four inches away from your body. It works well to sit at a table and rest your elbows on the edge. Don't sit too close to the table: if the pendulum is too close to your own body's energy field, the pendulum will receive interference, skewing your results. If the pendulum swings in a circular and clockwise direction, the test is positive and harmonious; if the pendulum

swings counter-clockwise the response is negative and dissonant. Once again, you can increase your accuracy by hiding the foods or supplements in small baggies or envelopes so you don't know specifically what it is you are testing.

It is possible to perform remote testing for others through self-testing, however, I would only advise this method for those readers who are knowledgeable, experienced and highly intuitive.

General Testing Instructions for Testing Another Person or Surrogate

**Always start a testing session by testing the arm strength in "neutral", that is without any influence other than your hand on their wrist. Ask the subject to think about the ceiling or some other neutral object while you push and test their resistance. This is the reference point and you can come back to it at any time to double-check and compare the weak, neutral and strong resistance.

**A strong muscle response is a positive response indicating that the subject is in harmony with the substance/issue being tested and that it is beneficial.

A weak muscle response is a negative response and indicates dissonance and that the substance/issue is of no benefit, and may even be detrimental.

A neutral response means that the muscle strength doesn't change and that the substance/issue is neither beneficial nor detrimental.

**Be sure to apply steady pressure for at least 1-2 seconds. Quite often, people will push and then release too quickly not giving the subject's arm time enough to respond.

**Use a gentle steady pressure and try not to bounce the arm.

**Don't apply pressure any further up the arm than the wrist. Otherwise the subject's resistance will become too strong.

**Depending on the subject's strength of resistance, you will need to adjust the pressure that you apply, otherwise you risk being too strong or too weak. You must learn to "match" your resistance to the strength of the person with whom you are working.

**If the subject offers too much resistance ask them to "lighten up" and be less rigid. Likewise, if the subject does not offer any or enough resistance, ask them to hold their arm more firmly. Some people like to brace their arm while others hold their arm like a limp noodle.

**Don't do any testing or energy work too close to electrical currents generated by computers, stoves, refrigerators, heaters, radios, televisions, etc. This will interfere with the results. Energy testing is best done several feet away from the nearest electrical appliance. It is best done indoors though, because when done outdoors energy flow is very difficult to contain and track. (If testing livestock, choose a sheltered area).

**Both the tester and the subject should remove all electrical devices such as watches, pagers and cell phones. Large pieces of jewelry should also be removed.

Troubleshooting

1) You can't tell if your subject's arm is strong or weak.

> Go back to the beginning and test their arm strength in *neutral*. To ensure that they are in neutral, simply ask them to think of nothing or about the ceiling. Then ask them to think of something they love – children, grandchildren, flowers, or home – and test their arm when you know it is strong. Then ask them to think of something they dislike – rain, cilantro, or rotten eggs – and feel the arm when it is weak. If your client's strength is still not well defined, remember to ask them to give you either more resistance or more flexibility, depending on what you need to determine the difference.

2) Energy testing doesn't seem to work for you and your results are inconsistent.

> Some students lack confidence in taking a leadership role and find it difficult to share their testing results and set their client up with a health program. If this is the case, start with simple tests and simple results and build your skills and your confidence slowly. Practice on as many different people and/or animals as you can. Study your area of interest or expertise to build knowledge and thereby confidence.

3) The person that you are working on is openly skeptical.

Energy testing works on skeptics too, however if they show lack of interest in the process or are treating it as a parlour game then it is advisable to wait until they are more receptive. Most skeptics however, are genuine in seeking help but are unable to change their current belief systems due to a lack of education or exposure to the topic at hand. Skepticism is bred by lack of knowledge; interestingly enough, very often the loudest skeptics have the least amount of information. Hard-core skeptics seem to believe in very little. Isn't it a lot more fun to believe in everything? The world can then be viewed as it is – a playground of fascinating experiences full of human and divine creations.

Avoid feeding skepticism; ignore their perceptions and stay focused on the energy work at hand. There is no need for verbal discussion to force them into your way of thinking. Allow them plenty of space to find their own way. The information that their sub-conscious gives you might be limited, but you should be able to get enough results to formulate a health program. Some of my most successful cases were people who *started* their healing journey as skeptics. Not surprisingly, you will find that the easiest people to work with, and therefore those that get the best results, are those who are very open to the process and simply allow energy and information to "flow".

Frequently Asked Questions...

1) What about Permission?
If anyone has asked you for help with their situation, then permission has already been granted. At that time there is no reason to bypass their conscious decision in an effort to dig up subconscious belief systems. However, if someone has asked you for help on another person's behalf, you should advise them to get that other person to contact you directly. Often the person in question is not yet serious about seeking help, which is why they have not come to you directly. Unless they are physically unable, never perform a health work-up on a person who has not indicated to you directly that this is what they want. And no matter who you want to help, always wait until you are asked. This is especially true for family, friends and loved ones – often you are desperate to give them some help but they have not embraced your health methods. Refrain from telling them what to do and don't allow yourself to get frustrated. The more you push, the farther they will move away. Lovingly give each person the space they need to make their own choices. We cannot possibly know what is best for another person at a particular time. A person who has not asked for help or is not ready to make changes will not respond to any kind of treatment, no matter how effective it could be. The way to help is through example: eat well; exercise; and maintain a positive attitude (no matter how adverse the circumstances). Be joyful and compassionate and the healing light will follow you everywhere.

Likewise, when working with small children and animals we must always wait until their guardian or caregiver has directly asked us for help. On occasion, a child or an animal will disagree with this decision and want to be left alone. It is my experience that if you move slowly and perhaps even sit with the subject for a time without doing anything other than just being, you will be able to gain their acceptance, trust and friendship, thereby making the healing journey a positive experience. Some people and/or animals feel vulnerable and don't like strangers invading their energy fields. In distance healings I've had dogs or horses try to bite me as soon as they sense my energy field close by. At that point I try to be as polite as I can by waiting patiently and quietly and giving them plenty of time to get to know me – that might take anywhere from one to thirty minutes. Be patient…I've never had one yet that didn't accept my help.

Be a Joyful and Compassionate Healer

2) Can Energy Testing be Performed from a Distance?

As discussed in Chapter 3 the world of energy is a world of light and information not bound by space or time. It makes no difference to the human or animal energy field whether or not they in the same room as you, or if they are in Singapore, or on the moon. You can formulate a successful program for a distant client with the help of your surrogate. In fact, remote testing and/or energy healings are often made easier without the presence of the dense energy field of the physical body.

3) Is it Necessary to Clear Your Own Energy Field?

It is recommended that you clear your own energy field before doing any work of this nature. You can clear your energy field by smudging (feather and smudge stick), using a clearing crystal or by stretching and shaking your body. If you are very focused and experienced, instruct yourself psychically to clear all unwanted negativities, obstructive emotions, judgments, or assumptions. You should always clear yourself in between sessions if you are working on people or animals in succession. (It is not necessary to clear the subject before working on them.)

Focus, Focus, Focus…

No matter what technique you are using the single most significant thing that will make the difference between average results and outstanding results is focus. Think about what you are testing: if the person is holding salt, think about salt; if you are testing the liver, try to visualize the liver organ itself; if you are running through a list of minerals, keep your mind on the mineral you are testing. And so on…the minute your focus becomes distracted, so will the results.

Focus and practice will eventually become medical intuition - an exciting new tool for your healing chest. And medical intuition will eventually become energy healing!

Let's Become Healers…

Now that we have discussed methods and techniques for practicing basic kinesiology, in Chapter 5 I'm going to teach you a very specific and thorough method for formulating successful health programs…*The Marijke Method*™.

Chapter 5

THE MARIJKE METHOD™
- Exceptional Results -

The Marijke Method™ was developed by the author over a period of more than two decades of study, practice, clinical experience and thousands upon thousands of successful cases. It is a four step method that allows for the accurate identification of organ imbalances, food allergies and intolerances, nutrient deficiencies, and for determining exactly which remedies will be of most benefit. The method allows for customizing a successful and specific health program that works. It's an easy system to learn, it's tidy and it's fun.

Intake & Observation

Before beginning a work-up on another person (or yourself), do a comprehensive intake. Be sure to ask lots of questions about the details of both current health problems and previous health conditions. Remember, you are a medical detective - intuition is more meaningful if you have information. Be a good listener: many times the client inadvertently answers their own questions in an interview. Be as thorough as you can.

Find out the following:
When did the condition begin? What season was it? Did they start any new medications or supplements? What is their current supplement program? Are they currently taking any

medications? Did the diet change? Did they move – buildings, houses or geography? Was there a change in environment – chemical, industrial or air quality? Were there changes at work? Did their personal lives change? Did any of their relationships change? What, if anything, are they addicted to? Were they under stress?

Use your powers of observation including facial expressions, body language and tone of voice. Are they asking for help for obvious problems or are they quietly seeking help for something deeper – usually emotional?

And last, do they really want to be there? Some people will consciously seek out help, as a result of family pressure or on the advice of friends for example – but in actual fact they have no intention of helping themselves. Even some people faced with terminal illnesses don't have a strong desire to live, although this truth may be deeply buried in the psyche.

Read the Client

Don't push people further than they can handle, or yourself for that matter. Whereas a dietary fast can easily be recommended to a health-conscious yoga instructor, the same recommendation to a "meat and potatoes" truck driver will scare her or him off permanently. Newcomers to natural health programs may have to be encouraged to eliminate one or two food groups to start, or perhaps all they can manage in the beginning is to quit drinking coffee. Be patient and allow such people (or yourself) to feel some benefits before asking them to do more.

Order of Go

To perform a comprehensive and thorough assessment leading to a successful natural health program, we will learn and follow the "order of go". Don't stray from the order of go, especially when you are first learning, as the results may not be accurate. The order of go ensures that the program is structured, thorough and eliminates the risk of confusion or the possibility of over-looking significant underlying causes of ill health. As well, the client's energy field will change and shift as you work through the layers because the healing energy is already moving. Staying focused on the order of go will ensure that you are in sync with these changes.

We are treating people, not health conditions. For example, ten different people with the same symptom profile of rheumatoid arthritis will each have a different nutritional program, depending on the uniqueness of the person – health history, health quality, biochemistry, nutritional status, lifestyle, and attitude. Drug therapy, on the other hand, will treat ten different rheumatoid arthritics with the same medication programs, usually based on the severity of their symptoms. Avoid falling into the same trap - don't get in the habit of treating conditions and stereotyping people because they have the same disease.

At no time do I want to discourage beginners from using any of the following methods, either for themselves or for others. However, there is a lot of information here and there is no harm in learning one step at a time and practicing them until you are feeling proficient. Even just working with Step 1 and Step

2 will bring miraculous results. Keep it simple, positive and fun – as healing should be!

Step 1 - Organ Testing

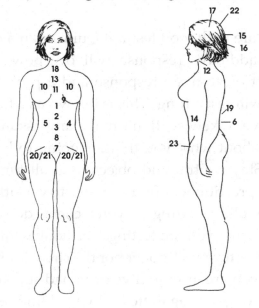

1. Stomach	6. Kidneys	12. Lymph	18. Thyroid
2. Small Intestine	7. Prostate	13. Thymus	19. Adrenals
3. Large Intestine	8. Bladder	14. Spleen	20. Ovaries
4. Pancreas	9. Heart	15. Hypothalamus	21. Testicles
5. Liver &	10. Lungs	16. Pituitary	22. Brain
Gallbladder	11. Bronchials	17. Pineal	23. Blood

See the Appendix for a full-size image of the Illustration of Testing Points.
See Chapter 6 for a complete description of organ function and physiology.

Organ testing is always the first step in the health work-up and you will begin by testing each point to identify imbalances. Organ points, meridian points and different body systems can be tested by using your free hand to point directly to the area of interest. You can physically touch it lightly or point at it using focus. Dysfunctional or diseased organs will cause a weak muscle response; a healthy organ and good energy flow will have a neutral or slightly stronger effect on the strength of the muscle.

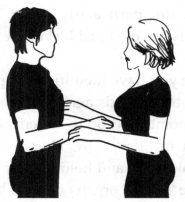

Don't try and determine the underlying cause or reason for any imbalances that you find. In other words, try not to reach any conclusions until the work-up is complete. Start by recording a weak, strong or neutral response for each organ point – see the Appendix for a checklist.

Step 2 - Food Testing

Start the second step by doing a general test for a variety of suspected foods. When doing a general test for a particular food, ask the subject to hold the food sample close to the sternum (when standing) or by laying the food on their abdomen (when lying down). This ensures focus and a close relationship with the test sample. If a food sample is detrimental the client's arm will lose strength and be weaker – the food does not have resonance. If a food is very beneficial the client's arm will become stronger than neutral its benefits are proportional to how much strength the muscle gains. If a food is neither damaging nor beneficial to the health of the body the arm strength will be neutral, i.e. neither weak nor strong. Keep a list of foods that test weak and any foods that are testing particularly strong. To record your results use the Food List in the Appendix.

Once you have identified the problem foods hold those foods against the imbalanced organ points and body systems that you identified in Step 1. In other words take each "weak" food and hold it on or over each one of the "weak" organ points. (There is no need to test foods against any organ points that tested strong in Step 1). A weak food response indicates that the food is creating symptoms and problems for that specific organ. A strong response indicates that the food is neutral.

If a food tests weak on the general test that you have just completed, but strong on a specific organ, that food should still be eliminated from the diet because the general test is indicating that this food is causing symptoms somewhere else in the body. For example, to determine if coffee is causing a person's heart palpitations, place or hold a coffee sample over the heart and test their muscle strength. Whereas the caffeine may have tested weak on the general body test, it may very well test strong when tested on the heart, meaning that it is not contributing to the cause of heart distress but could perhaps be causing insomnia. Results can be unexpected - keep an open mind and be ready for lots of interesting surprises!

Test all suspected foods on one point before moving on, rather than testing one food at a time on every unbalanced point. This maintains focus and flow.

I would recommend that you make a "test kit" by putting a variety of foods in a sepa-

rate container such as a small vial, especially the foods discussed in Chapter 2. You do not have to remove the food sample from the vial for testing purposes.

Be aware with food testing! Quite often a client's addictive response will overpower a correct or accurate response and a problem food will test strong. This is known as a false positive. Likewise, don't make any assumptions about what you think is going to happen. Stay neutral and objective at all times! Some practitioners find it easier to do either single blind testing – your client doesn't know what you are testing – or double blind – neither the practitioner nor the client knows what you are testing. (I've even had smokers test strong to a cigarette in double blind tests – such is the power of the addictive subconscious!) As a beginner, in order to avoid these pitfalls I would suggest using the single blind method…and remember to stay focused.

"Let thy food be thy medicine and thy medicine be thy food"
…Hippocrates

Step 3 – Testing Nutrient Status

Now that all of the points have been tested and it is determined which foods should be eliminated from the diet, we will test every unbalanced organ point for nutrient deficiencies. (Don't bother testing the healthy organ points for nutrient imbalances.)

We will be testing four different nutrient groups:
1) Vitamins
2) Minerals

3) Essential fatty acids
4) Nutraceuticals.

Let's start with vitamins as the first group:

While accessing the organ point with your hand or finger(s), (either touch it physically or point at it with focus) you will test the energy between that particular organ and all vitamins. The easiest way to do this is verbally – focus on all vitamins as a group, then test the specific point while saying the word "vitamins" out loud. A weak response indicates an imbalance in the vitamin group; at this point that's all it indicates: it may either be a deficiency or an excess.

Now we need to determine which vitamin is unbalanced. While accessing the point with fingers or focus, test each vitamin by calling it out verbally (see Appendix for the list of vitamins). Record those that elicit a weak response. In most cases this will indicate a deficiency unless the subject is already supplementing with that vitamin and perhaps getting too much. Before you begin ALWAYS ask for a list of the supplements that the subject is currently taking. Obviously, a nutrient that is in excess should be discontinued.

You will use exactly the same process for the minerals. However, if essential fatty acids and/or nutraceuticals come up weak those categories cannot be tested as individual deficiencies since they are considered supplements rather than naturally occurring nutrients present in the body. Instead you will test them as supplements as instructed in Step 4 – Supplement Testing.

Don't try to do the verbal testing too quickly. Give the client time to respond as you call out the name of the nutrient. Remember, you are always testing energetic imbalances between the organ point and the nutrient. Do not ask yes or no questions like, "Is Vitamin C good for her?" or "Will Vitamin B12 make my liver feel better?" *Just test the resonance or dissonance between the energy field of the nutrient and the energy field of the organ.*

You can make a complete test kit containing samples of each nutrient (vitamins, minerals, essential fatty acids and nutraceuticals) but it is not convenient to individually physically test each and every one vitamin to determine deficiencies or excesses. Rather, I would recommend using actual samples to validate your results at the end. Testing the sample itself should elicit a very strong response in the case of a corrected nutrient deficiency.

Step 4 - Supplement Testing

One of the most significant benefits of energy testing is the ability to determine which remedies, herbs and supplements in the vast jungle of products out there are most likely to help the client. Since there are hundreds, if not thousands, of different supplements to choose from, energy testing is an excellent method for cutting through the confusion. And no, it is not necessary to test hundreds of products. Rather, this book will read as a guide to those remedies and herbs that are most beneficial in most health situations - see Chapters 8 and 9. Always be creative however, and use your intuition to lead you to other possible remedies that could help resolve the problem.

Once again, it's a good idea to make a "test kit" of the most common herbs and supplements but the technique can work well with verbal testing too. If you have the sample then test it by holding it next to the organ point and determining the benefit in the same way as the food testing was done. A strong response is beneficial and a weak response is detrimental, or at least of no benefit.

ALWAYS, always be sure to test any supplements, nutrients, herbs or remedies that the person is already taking. Hold it directly to the problem area to determine if it contributing to the problem. Very often the person is reacting to something in their supplement program, especially anything that they have been taking for several weeks or months. These people have usually seen multiple doctors or other practitioners never realizing that there was a simple solution. I've seen chronic fevers in a woman who had been taking feverfew for several months for her migraine headaches; I've seen bone pain and severe muscle pain in women who take vitamin D for too long (which can cause excessively high calcium levels); I've seen acute neck pain resulting from a patient's reaction to magnesium stearate, a key ingredient in most supplement capsules; and I've seen several cases of chronic insomnia caused by iron supplements. And on…and on…and on…

You can test for dosages for supplements but if you are inexperienced and/or unfamiliar with certain supplements I recommend always following the directions on the product package.

**Remember, you are not asking the body whether or not it needs anything. Do NOT ask questions. You are simply testing the energies or polarities between the organ points and the supplements. A weak response shows no benefits; a strong response indicates that it is of benefit. You are always looking for harmony or disharmony, not yes or no answers (as we discussed in Chapter 3).

Remember, a positive response is always beneficial; a negative response is detrimental

Let's Do an Example
Step 1 - Organ Testing
Test results show that the left lobe of the thyroid is weak.

Step 2 – Food Testing
After testing several foods by touching the thyroid with food samples you find a weak reading for coffee, cheese and milk and you identify caffeine and dairy products as foods that aggravate the thyroid.

Step 3 – Nutrient Testing
When you test the thyroid's general nutrient status for vitamins, minerals, essential fatty acids and nutraceuticals, there is a weak reading for both vitamins and minerals and a neutral reading for essential fatty acids and nutraceuticals. After verbally testing each individual vitamin you find that there is a weak reading for vitamin B6. Likewise, after testing each separate mineral you find a weak reading for selenium.

The client reports that they are currently not

taking either the Vitamin B6 or the selenium, thus ruling out an excess. You have now determined that the thyroid is deficient for both vitamin B6 and selenium. If you have the physical samples of vitamin B6 and/or selenium samples on hand, you can validate your results by holding them (one at a time) on the thyroid point and testing the body's response. They should both test very strongly.

Step 4 – Supplement Testing
Based on the information in Chapter 7, you test the thyroid for Oregon grape root, ashwaghanda and homeopathic thyroid. Only the ashwaghanda tests "strong", so you determine that this is the most beneficial herb to use at this time.

The example program formulated for the thyroid from the Four-Step *Marijke Method*™ is as follows:

No dairy products
No caffeine
Vitamin B6
Selenium
Ashwaghanda

Healing is Simply Natural

Determining Relationships Between Organs
Once you are feeling proficient with the Order of Go, it can also be useful to determine if there is a relationship between the primary problem area and any other body system or organ that is contributing to the symptoms. This holistic technique allows you to work with any underlying causes found in a secondary area. For example, let's say you are dealing with a chronic ear infection that has been stubborn to treatment. You suspect a link between the ear symptoms and liver toxicity based on your results in Step 1. Draw an energetic line with your free hand between the affected ear and the liver point to see if the link tests weak. If it does test weak, this indicates that liver toxins are directly influencing the ear symptoms and that establishing a cleansing program for the liver will help to heal the ear.

Use General Diet Plans
Even though we can identify very specific food problems with *The Marijke Method*™ we often need to determine which overall diet or food plan is most likely to be of benefit for a particular person with a particular health condition. Along with food eliminations, specific diet plans often get results very quickly and perform miracles!

Bear in mind that our nutritional dietary requirements can change very quickly and that our diets may need to be adjusted frequently, especially when the body is healing. A diet that worked a few months ago will not necessarily work the same today. Our bodies are in a continual state of flux – *as a healing body should be!* Our bodies crave variety in food…just as they do in life.

To test specific diets and cleanses, use the Diet Plan list and instructions in Chapter 7.

Food is Power

A Word of Caution

Of course, if people have chronic and/or re-occurring symptoms and are not responding to a program of diet, nutrients and remedies ensure that they have completed a full conventional medical evaluation in order to uncover any other serious contributing factors or causes. Although, usually people with challenging problems have already been through a series of medical tests with uncertain results, which then motivates them to seek help elsewhere.

So let's get on with the exciting business of learning about organ points, their function, their corrections and their significance on a successful healing journey...

Chapter 6

TESTING ORGAN POINTS and BODY SYSTEMS
-The Body Talks: Food; Nutrients; Remedies and Emotions-

Body Wisdom

Consider that each organ as a being unto itself with its own physical, emotional and spiritual needs. Recognize that these organs and body systems require loving attention just like you do and that they are working together like finely tuned machine pieces for the health and balance and common good of one major engine – you! Everything that happens to your body is created by you through your lifestyle, your belief systems, and the blueprints in your energy field (read soul). No matter whether it is a skin lesion, a headache, a sore elbow or a tumour, the cells have responded to messages and signals from the central nervous system. Do *not* act like a victim; your body has not *done* this to you – it is doing it *for* you. Respect its wisdom. The un-wellness has been created through one or more complex factors, including physical toxicity, conscious and subconscious belief systems, karma, deep-seated psychological patterns and/or stress.

The physical body is truly more than the sum of its parts. Each part is a microcosm – little worlds of a higher and expanded consciousness connected to the "whole" of your physical, emotional, mental and spiritual body. It is a place of fascinating function, cooperation and divine harmony, driven by the power of love.

Body Testing Basics

In this chapter the discussion of each organ and body system includes a guideline to the most common food intolerances and nutrient deficiencies as well as beneficial supplements and homeopathic remedies that, in the twenty years of my natural health practice, I have found to have the most significant effect on the specific body organs and systems.

Keep in mind though, that as comprehensive as this guideline is, that any food can cause a reaction in *any* part of the body, *any* deficiency can emerge, and many other supplements, other than those I have mentioned, may also be of benefit. Therefore, don't hesitate to test any items outside of these recommendations.

Be sure to test all supplements that a person is already taking: many times the adverse effects of the supplements themselves, no matter how healthy they seem, can be the underlying cause of symptoms.

Be aware of drugs – over-the-counter, prescription and/or street – they have the potential to cause a wide variety of symptoms. Even with pharmaceuticals, whether or not the symptom is documented as a known adverse side effect is not relevant. People and their response to drugs are very unique.

For the bi-lateral organs – kidneys, adrenals, thyroid, ovaries, testes, lungs – ensure that both the right and left sides are tested separately.

The guideline also includes specific emotions that I have often found stored in different organs. These emotions always contribute, in varying degrees, to an overall health imbalance. However, emotions other than the ones listed, can be found in these same organs as well; people are unique and there are no rules. See "Emotional Kinesiology" at the end of the chapter.

Advanced Body Testing

To keep it simple, each organ is tested as one general point. In other words, you are testing the health of the overall stomach or the health of the overall liver. However, I have added "Advanced Test Points" for more in-depth testing, which allows experienced readers to determine very specific imbalances in that particular organ. See the Appendix for details on working with Advanced Test Points.

"Supporting organs" are those organs that work in close relationship with the organ being tested. Supporting organs are the organs most likely to affect the health of the organ in question and should therefore be carefully considered as a possible contributing factor, either directly or indirectly. I have included them here to emphasize the relationship between the different organs.

Neither one of these methods are necessary in order to complete a comprehensive work-up with effective results. So let's get started and have fun!

Keep It Simple

• Test each potential food problem for a weak muscle response by holding the food item next to the organ point.
• Test each nutrient for a positive muscle response by holding the nutrient next to the

organ point.

• Test each supplement for a positive muscle response by holding the supplement next to the organ point.

• Test homeopathic remedies for a positive muscle response by holding the remedy next to the organ point.

• Test each emotion for a weak muscle response by calling out the emotion verbally.

All of these foods, supplements and remedies can be tested verbally however it is beneficial to use physical test samples for foods, nutrients and remedies as it strengthens the test results.

Remember, a positive response is always beneficial; a negative response is detrimental

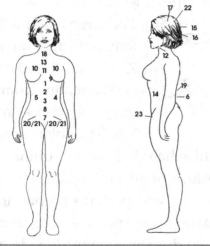

1. Stomach	6. Kidneys	12. Lymph	18. Thyroid
2. Small Intestine	7. Prostate	13. Thymus	19. Adrenals
3. Large Intestine	8. Bladder	14. Spleen	20. Ovaries
4. Pancreas	9. Heart	15. Hypothalamus	21. Testicles
5. Liver & Gallbladder	10. Lungs	16. Pituitary	22. Brain
	11. Bronchials	17. Pineal	23. Blood

See the Appendix for a full-size image of the Illustration of Testing Points. To test skin, bones, teeth and muscles simply touch the area in question while performing the muscle test.

Gastrointestinal

Stomach

The stomach is a J-shaped distensible organ whose primary functions are to serve as a mixing vat and a reservoir, and to partially digest proteins - mainly from meat. Protein digestion occurs through the secretion of hydrochloric acid (HCL) and pepsin. Gastric indigestion symptoms such as heartburn, belching, reflux and ulcers are most commonly caused by caffeine, which suppresses HCL production, and by excess carbohydrate ingestion which causes the fermentation of starches and sugars to produce acids, heat and toxins. Contrary to popular belief stomach indigestion is not caused by high HCL levels, but by low HCL levels combined with high levels of volatile fatty acids. Unfriendly bacteria (e.g. Helicobacter pylori) and yeast thrive in these toxic conditions, leading to the secretion of more toxins and subsequent damage to the stomach lining. Therefore, a diet high in bread, pasta, baked goods and pizza is one of the major causes of stomach problems.

Problem Foods – caffeine, sugar, wheat, oats, rye, barley, rice, dairy products, beef, eggs
Common Nutrient Deficiencies – potassium, folic acid, iodine, calcium, magnesium
Beneficial Supplements –vinegar (red wine or apple cider), probiotics, ginger, aloe vera, peppermint, mastica chios (gum mastica), comfrey leaf, licorice root, marshmallow root, gentian
Homeopathic Remedies – nux-vomica, pulsatilla, sulphur

Emotions – fear, anxiety, overwhelm
Advanced Test Points – HCL and pepsin production, integrity of the interior mucus membranes, bacteria, yeast and parasites.
Supporting Organs – small intestine, large colon

Small Intestine

The small intestine is a 3 metre long tube with a 1 inch diameter joining the stomach to the large colon. The stomach releases liquid food material into the small intestine; it does so in small quantities so as not to overload it. Almost all digestion and absorption of food nutrients into the bloodstream occurs in the small intestine. It is divided into 3 sections: the duodenum; jejunum and ileum. (Intestinal ulcers are normally found in the duodenum.) The small intestine is lined with microvilli that serve to increase the surface area of the entire intestinal membrane. These villi secrete several digestive enzymes which, together with pancreatic enzymes and bile (see below) break down partially digested carbohydrates, proteins and lipids into smaller units (sugars, peptides and fatty acids respectively) which are then passed into the bloodstream or lymphatic system.

A person with gluten intolerances often sustains damage to the villi in the small intestine that interferes with the absorption of nutrients from food. This causes a variety of food intolerance symptoms as discussed in Chapter 2.

Problem Foods – sugar, wheat, oats, rye, barley, rice, dairy products, beef, caffeine
Common Nutrient Deficiencies – folic acid, iodine, calcium, magnesium
Beneficial Supplements - vinegar (red wine or apple cider), probiotics, ginger, aloe vera, peppermint, mastica chios (gum mastica), comfrey leaf, licorice root, marshmallow root, gentian
Homeopathic Remedies – nux vomica, lycopodium, china
Emotions – insecurity, lack of confidence, rejection
Advanced Test Points - digestive enzymes, integrity of the mucus membranes, microvilli, Peyer's patches (lymph tissue), bacteria, yeast and parasites
Supporting Organs – large colon

Large Intestine (Colon)

The large colon is 1.5 metres long with a 2.5 inch diameter. Any mal-digested or undigested matter from the small intestine passes into the colon. The colon acts as a septic field where billions of strains of friendly bacteria ferment any of the *undigested* carbohydrates and proteins preparing them for elimination. This process of fermentation releases hydrogen, carbon dioxide and methane gases. Therefore, the passage of too many mal-digested foods into the colon causes excess fermentation and the production of toxic by-products. This leads to gas, heat and acid build-up. This imbalance in the colonic ecosystem creates an environment of toxicity, killing off friendly bacteria and encouraging the growth of pathogenic bacteria, yeast and parasites. The combination of heat, acids and toxins damages the lining of the mucus membranes making it abnormally permeable and allowing the migration of acids, pathogens and toxins into the various body systems. This is known as "leaky gut" - it is an intestinal epidemic, responsible for a host of health conditions and diseases (see Chapter 2). Furthermore, the colon has the largest blood supply of any organ in the body - no wonder! - a huge volume of blood is required to transport *all* of these toxins to the liver for detoxification. A toxic colon equals a toxic liver. The colon likes well digested food and lots of fibre. It doesn't like sugar, refined carbohydrates, excess meat or rancid fats.

Problem Foods – sugar, wheat, oats, rye, barley, rice, dairy products, beef, high fat foods
Common Nutrient Deficiencies – vitamin B12, folic acid, iron, iodine
Beneficial Supplements - probiotics, psyllium seed, slippery elm, garlic, crushed flax seeds, bentonite clay, aloe vera, kelp, chlorophyll, fibre supplements
Homeopathic Remedies – nux-vomica, sulphur, lycopodium
Emotions – fear, anxiety, self-hatred, relationship stress, rejection
Advanced Test Points - leaky gut, bacteria, yeast, parasites and probiotic levels
Supporting Organs – liver

Pancreas

The pancreas has two significant functions. It produces up to 1.5 litres of pancreatic juice daily, containing several digestive enzymes as well as sodium bicarbonate (baking soda) that buffers the acidity in the entire small intestine. The enzymes continue to digest carbohydrates, proteins and fats, preparing them for absorption from the small intestine into the bloodstream and lymphatics. The pancreas also secretes insulin, a hormone that functions to open up receptors in the muscles and liver, allowing blood sugar to enter the tissues for energy. A lack of insulin or non-responsive receptors determines diabetes (high blood sugar).

Problem Foods – sugar, wheat, oats, rye, barley, rice, dairy products, beef, excess fat
Common Nutrient Deficiencies – chromium, magnesium, manganese, zinc, alpha-lipoic acid
Beneficial Supplements – digestive enzymes, licorice root, juniper berry, dandelion root, cinnamon, spirulina
Homeopathic Remedies – alfalfa, lycopodium, insulin, pancreas, uranium nitricum, syzgium
Emotions – frustration, deadline worry, over-work, stress of any kind
Advanced Test Points – beta cells (secrete insulin), individual digestive enzymes (lipase, sucrase, amylase and lactase)
Supporting Organs – adrenals, liver, pituitary

Liver and Gallbladder

The liver is the second largest organ in the body (after the skin) and has numerous functions. The liver metabolizes carbohydrates by breaking down glycogen into glucose, used for energy throughout the body. As well, it converts glu-

85

cose back into glycogen for storage. The liver also completes the breakdown of protein so that the amino acids can be used for energy. This process results in toxic ammonia, which is then converted into less toxic urea to be eliminated in the urine.

The liver secretes up to 1 litre of bile (containing bile salts) daily, which is used as a vehicle for excreting toxins and debris. These toxins are a result of the liver's function as a detoxifier of drugs, chemicals, poisons, environmental toxins, bacterial products, food antigens and cecal toxins – 80% of the liver's blood supply comes from the colon for purification. The liver is an important part of the immune response and plays a key role in defending the body against pathogens (including bacteria and viruses) and it acts as an organ barrier or filter between the digestive system and the rest of the body. As well, it stores certain nutrients such as vitamins A, D, E and B12; iron, coenzyme Q10, selenium and copper. The liver also metabolizes hormones, such as thyroid, estrogen and testosterone. This is why the liver is of such importance in hormonal imbalances and hormone related cancers.

The gallbladder is a pear-shaped sac that hangs below the liver. It serves as a storehouse for bile and is stimulated by various hormones to release the bile into the small intestine to emulsify and allow for the absorption of dietary fats. The liver uses cholesterol to synthesize bile salts. If the bile contains insufficient bile salts or excessive cholesterol, gallstones will form and are capable of causing a variety of digestive symptoms - nausea, vomiting, bloating, excess gas and indigestion.

Problem Foods – caffeine (a powerful drug that is contraindicated in all liver conditions), excess fats, excess meat, dairy products, sugar, wheat, low fibre, alcohol, prescription drugs

Common Nutrient Deficiencies – vitamins B12, B6, and C, selenium, iron, coenzyme Q10, sulphur

Beneficial Supplements – goldenseal, milk thistle, dandelion root, astragalus, garlic, kelp, yellow dock, chanca piedra (gallstones), olive oil

Useful Therapies – castor oil packs (liver detox and gallstones - see Appendix)

Homeopathic Remedies – hepatine, nux-vomica, sulphur, lycopodium

Emotions – liver: anger; gallbladder: lack of confidence, inability to make decisions

Advanced Test Points – drug residue, fatty liver, bile flow, bacteria, viruses, yeast

Supporting Organs –large colon, blood

Kidneys, Bladder and Prostate

Kidneys and Bladder

The kidneys are complex organs responsible for filtering and detoxifying the blood and then forming urine, which is released into the bladder for storage. The urine excretes waste such as drugs, ammonia, urea, creatine (from the breakdown of muscle) and uric acid. The kidneys also reabsorb water, sugar and amino acids from protein. The kidneys regulate the blood levels of sodium, potassium, calcium, phosphate and chloride, regulate blood volume and blood pressure by conserving or eliminating water, and regulate blood ph (acidity) and blood glucose. They secrete a variety of hormones to activate these functions, including renin (blood pressure), anti-diuretic hormone (water regulation) and angiotensin (blood pressure). Factors that adversely affect kidney function include drugs, excess alcohol, toxic liver, excess protein (meat) and high sugar diets. The more toxic the liver is, the more toxins the kidneys are forced to filter – which they are not equipped to do over a long period of time.

Problem Foods – caffeine, alcohol, meat, salt, sugar, dairy products
Common Nutrient Deficiencies – potassium, sulphur, vitamin B6
Beneficial Supplements – juniper berry, horsetail, cranberry, yarrow, uva ursi, goldenseal, marshmallow root, parsley, lemon juice
Homeopathic Remedies – equisetum, berberis vulgaris, lycopodium, nux-vomica, hydrastis, ferr phos, apis, cantharis
Emotions – lack of self-importance, extreme stress, attention-seeking
Advanced Test Points – bladder, urethra, right and left ureters, bacteria, yeast, drug residue, toxins
Supporting Organs – liver, heart

Prostate

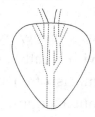

The prostate gland is a donut-shaped gland that lies just below the urinary bladder and above the penis – about the size of a walnut. The prostate secretes a milky, slightly acidic fluid that combines with a more alkaline seminal fluid produced by the seminal vesicles to form semen. The testicles produce sperm which is mixed with the semen. The sperm-rich fluid is then ejaculated during orgasm. Part of the urethra is found in the centre of the donut as it carries urine from the bladder to the penis. If the prostate enlarges it will pressure the urethra and constrict the flow of urine resulting in difficult, weak, frequent or painful urination. It may also interfere with erection.

Because the prostate is governed by hormones, the primary therapy for the prevention and treatment of prostate enlargement and prostate cancer is nutrition. Testosterone is converted into dihydrotestosterone (DHT) and one of the effects of excess DHT is to enlarge the prostate. It also causes male pattern baldness. Red meat, dairy products and caffeine all lead to high levels of DHT.

Problem Foods – caffeine, beef, pork, dairy products, excess fat, low fibre
Common Nutrient Deficiencies – zinc, iodine, essential fatty acids, Vitamin B6, vitamin E, lycopene
Beneficial Supplements – probiotics, flax seed, evening primrose oil, saw palmetto, kelp, pygeum, ginseng, licorice root, fibre
Homeopathic Remedies – testes, nux-vomica
Emotions – suppression, frustration
Advanced Test Points – bacteria, yeast
Supporting Organs – testes

Heart and Lungs

Heart

The heart is a very strong muscle that pumps more than 15,000 litres of blood per day. It is approximately the size of a fist and is located between the lungs, slightly to the left of the breastbone. De-oxygenated blood returns in the veins to the receiving chamber of the right side of the heart (atrium), passes through the tricuspid valve into the right ventricle, which pumps it into the lungs where it releases carbon dioxide and absorbs oxygen. The oxygenated blood is returned to the receiving chamber of the left side of the heart (atrium) via the pulmonary veins, passes through the mitral valve into the left ventricle. The left ventricle then pumps the blood through the aortic valve into the aorta, the largest artery of the body. The aorta then delivers the blood to the organs, tissues, and cells of the body, thereby delivering oxygen and nutrients to all its cells and then removing carbon dioxide and waste products made by those cells.

The heart itself must be nourished by a continuing supply of oxygen and nutrients which are transported through the heart's own arteries – the coronary arteries. It is these arteries that are so often at risk for partial or total blockages, resulting in chest pain that can spread to the neck, shoulders or left arm. Other symptoms include shortness of breath, lightheadedness, fainting, sweating, nausea, anxiety, irregular pulse, pale face and/or a feeling of impending doom. Any of these symptoms should be considered a medical emergency.

Problem Foods – excess fat, excess meat, sugar, caffeine, alcohol, dairy products
Common Nutrient Deficiencies – potassium, magnesium, calcium, iron; vitamins B6, silica, B12, E, folic acid, Coenzyme Q10; essential fatty acids (fish oils), carnitine
Beneficial Supplements – hawthorne, cayenne pepper, garlic, seripeptidase
Homeopathic Remedies – crategus, naja
Emotions – disappointed love, rejection of love, grief, loss, lack of emotional warmth, inability to bond with humans and/or animals
Advanced Test Points – tricuspid valve, mitral valve, aortic valve, coronary arteries, carotid arteries, bacteria, yeast, virus
Supporting Organs – arteries, liver, large colon

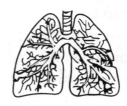

Lung and Bronchials
The lungs receive de-oxygenated blood from both the pulmonary arteries and the bronchial arteries. Upon inspiration, air travels down the main bronchial trunk which divides into smaller branches inside the lungs. The lungs, in tiny air sacs called alveoli, absorb oxygen from inhaled air and release carbon dioxide, a waste gas from the metabolism of food. From there the alveoli re-oxygenate the blood, which is then carried to the heart through the pulmonary veins. The carbon dioxide travels back up through the lungs and is expelled through the breath.

In asthma, the bronchial tubes inflame, swell, or spasm causing difficulty with breathing by blocking the airways. Asthma is often triggered by either food or inhalant allergies.
Bronchitis is characterized by coughing, wheezing, congestion of mucus, shortness of breath and chest pain. It is frequently a result of bacterial or viral infections, although

chronic bronchitis is typically caused by cigarette smoking - as is emphysema whereby the tobacco smoke damages the delicate alveoli. The alveoli then become much less efficient at processing the exchange of oxygen and carbon dioxide, leading to chronic breathing difficulties.

Problem Foods – dairy products, sugar, wheat, citrus, eggs, beef, sulphites, sulphur-based preservatives, (beware of glucosamine sulphate as the sulphate molecule can cause allergy reactions)

Inhalant allergies – dust, molds, pollens, feathers, trees (cedar, alder, birch, pine, poplar)

Common Nutrient Deficiencies – iron, iodine, selenium, zinc, vitamin A, beta-carotene, essential fatty acids (evening primrose oil, fish oils)

Beneficial Supplements – licorice root, lobelia, astragalus, fenugreek,

Homeopathic Remedies – kali carb, bryonia, nux-vomica, sulphur

Emotions – sadness, grief, dejection, disappointment

Advanced Test Points – right and left lobes, bronchioles, alveoli

Supporting Organs – adrenal glands, large colon

Immune System

The immune system is the body's defense against infectious organisms and any substances that the immune system has identified as foreign invaders – bacteria, viruses, and yeast for example. The immune system is extremely complex and involves a number of immune cells, proteins, tissues and hormones. The immune cells are white blood cells (leukocytes) and are produced in the lymphoid organs – thymus, spleen and bone marrow. They are then transported to the lymph nodes, which are found throughout various parts of the body. From here they circulate between the nodes and body organs to patrol the condition of the body, especially during episodes of invasion, infection, injury or tumour formation.

The two basic types of leukocytes are phagocytes, which destroy invaders, and lymphocytes, that both identify and destroy invaders. B cells and T cells are lymphocytes that are produced in the bone marrow. B lymphocytes produce antibodies which are specialized proteins that identify and then lock on to any dangerous invaders, known as antigens. While the antibodies don't kill the antigens, they are able to neutralize toxins and activate other parts of the immune system. It is also the antibodies' job to remember the type of invader in case of future attacks. This is why many infectious diseases, such as measles for example, can only strike once. It is the T cells that are known as the killer cells because it is their job to destroy any organisms identified by the B cells as antigens.

Antigens that induce an allergic reaction are known as allergens. Common allergens include air-borne particles (pollens, dust and molds), food allergies, poisons (insect or plant) drugs, vaccines, chemicals, tumour cells, or even the body's own tissues, in the case of auto-immune diseases.

Lymph, Thymus and Spleen

The lymphatic system is a series of channels

filled with clear lymphatic fluid. Lymph nodes act as filters or traps for impurities, toxins, bacteria, viruses, fats, mucus and foreign materials and are found in most parts of the body including the neck, throat, breast, intestines, groin and liver. The body actually has more lymphatic fluid than blood. Unlike the blood, however, it does not have a heart to circulate it. Therefore, lymphatic fluid must rely on exercise to pump it out of the kidneys. Exercise is therefore a key part of any detoxification and immunity-building program. Lymphatic congestion can be caused by improperly digested foods and poor bowel management. The lymphatic system gets clogged up and then diseases develop because of stagnant fluid. When this fluid does not circulate properly, the lymph nodes begin to retain waste materials.

The thymus gland is a double-lobed gland located in the upper chest behind the sternum. It is a primary immune organ because it produces billions of both B-cells and T-cells that carry out major immune responses. The thymus gland produces several hormones – thymosin, thymic humoral factor (THF), thymic factor (TF) and thymopoietin – all of which promote the proliferation of the T-cells to destroy microbes and foreign substances. The thymus gland is much larger in children, and shrinks considerably with age. Nevertheless its functions remain significant in maintaining a healthy adult immune system that is resistant to chronic disease and allergies. During acute stress, this gland shrinks to half its size within a day: millions of lymphocytes are destroyed and the immune system plummets.

During acute stress the thymus gland shrinks to half its size within a day

The spleen is the largest mass of lymphatic tissue in the body, containing both B-cells and T-cells and macrophages that ingest antigens and old and diseased red blood cells. The spleen is therefore a major player in the immune defense team. The spleen also removes damaged red blood cells from the bloodstream and saves any iron stored in these cells (in the form of ferritin or bilirubin) and then returns the iron to the bone marrow. Iron is a major element of hemoglobin, a blood protein that carries oxygen. The spleen is also able to act as a reservoir for stored blood, returning it to the general circulation when needed, as in the case of trauma for example.

Problem Foods – dairy products, glutens, nightshades (potatoes, tomatoes, peppers), nuts, excess fat, all specific food allergens
Common Nutrient Deficiencies – zinc, beta-carotene, vitamin C, iodine, iron, calcium
Beneficial Supplements – astragalus, reishi, shiitake, pau d'arco, echinacea, oregon grape root, goldenseal
Homeopathic Remedies – thymus, thymuline, spleen, lymph, sulphur, silicea
Emotions – acute or chronic stress of any kind, hidden or sub-conscious fears, hot temper (spleen)
Advanced Test Points – lymph nodes (tonsils, neck, groin, armpit, liver), bacteria, viruses, yeast, food allergies, parasites
Supporting Organs – adrenals, liver

Endocrine System

The endocrine system is comprised of a number of organs that release hormones into the bloodstream: pineal, hypothalamus, pituitary, thyroid, thymus, adrenals, ovaries and testes. These organs work together synergistically and all the hormones function as a team. Hormones are delivered to virtually every cell in the body where they regulate muscle activity, alter metabolism, control growth and development, balance energy, help with immunity and influence the operation of reproductive processes. Together with the nervous system, the endocrine system coordinates the functions of all body systems.

Hormone secretion is regulated by:
1) Signals from the nervous system (e.g. anxiety releases adrenaline)
2) Chemical changes in the blood (e.g. high blood sugar triggers the release of insulin)
3) Other hormones (e.g. pituitary ACTH stimulates adrenal cortisol production)

A given hormone only affects specific target cells: the target cells have receptors that bind and recognize the hormones. Receptors regulate hormone intake by decreasing or increasing their responsiveness, depending on whether or not the hormone is in excess or is deficient. A target cell has 2,000 - 100,000 receptors for a particular hormone.

The most common endocrine disorders involve either inadequate or excessive release of a hormone. Whereas conventional medicine generally considers that the endocrine organ itself is faulty (as they do with most body systems) and must be supported through drug intervention (or surgery), we will explore a variety of underlying causes (mostly dietary and nutritional) that are easy to correct.

Aside from the foods listed, caffeine should be considered an absolute poison to any endocrine gland disorder; it will interfere with both hormone production, secretion and reception. Nicotine will do the same.

> *Caffeine should be considered an absolute poison to the hormone system, as should nicotine*

Hypothalamus

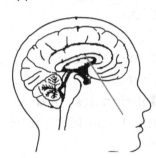

The hypothalamus is a very small region of the brain above the pituitary and is considered the "master" gland since it secretes several different hormones that control all the other endocrine glands, via the pituitary. It secretes thyrotropin-releasing hormone (TRH), prolactin-releasing hormone (PRH), gonadotropin-releasing hormone (GnRH), growth hormone-releasing hormone (GHRH), corticotropin-releasing hormone (CRH), somatostatin (growth hormone inhibiting hormone (GHIH), and dopamine (prolactin inhibiting hormone – PIH). All of these hormones are released into the bloodstream and immediately travel to the anterior lobe of the pituitary gland which then uses them to control and regulate all other hormones in the body. TRH, GnRH, GHRH, CRH and PRH stimulate pituitary gland secretion and the GHIH and PIH inhibit or suppress pituitary gland secretion. The hypothalamus also secretes anti-diuretic hormone (ADH) and oxytocin which are delivered to the posterior lobe of the pituitary. All of these hormones are secreted in periodic bursts.

The hypothalamus is the major integrating link between the nervous and endocrine systems. It receives information from several regions of the brain. Therefore pain, stress and emotions all cause changes in hypothalamic activity, controlling the nervous system, body temperature, thirst, hunger, sexual behaviour and the "fight and flight" reactions of rage and fear. The hypothalamus also determines our personal motivation.

Problem Foods – caffeine, sugar, dairy products, wheat, alcohol
Common Nutrient Deficiencies – iodine, zinc, selenium, vitamins B6 and B12, folic acid
Beneficial Supplements – evening primrose oil, fish oils
Homeopathic Remedies – hypothalamus
Emotions – any or all of them but particularly fear and anger
Advanced Test Points – all the releasing hormones – TRH, PRH, GnRH, GHRH, CRH, GHIH, PIH
Supporting Organs – brain, adrenals

Pituitary

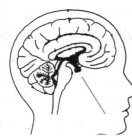

The pituitary gland is a small bean-shaped organ that hangs down from the lower center of the brain on a stalk attached to the hypothalamus.

However, the size of this little gland is completely incongruent with its significant role as a major hormone producer. The pituitary is stimulated by the hypothalamus via the releasing hormones listed above and then synthesizes and releases seven different types of pituitary gland hormones in the anterior (front) lobe. These hormones then stimulate the other endocrine glands (thyroid, adrenals, kidneys, ovaries and testes) to secrete their specific hormones. This makes the pituitary a "master gland", second only to the hypothalamus. The posterior (back) lobe does not synthesize hormones, but it does store and release two hormones – oxytocin and anti-diuretic hormone.

Kinesiology can be of great benefit in assessing pituitary function since standard medical blood tests are not particularly accurate. Pituitary hormones are also released in short bursts with no secretion in between bursts and the hormones are quickly used once secreted. With increasing stimulation, the hormone concentration in blood increases; in the absence of stimulation, the concentration decreases. Thus, the hormone level in the blood at any given moment does not indicate whether production is normal over the course of a day. Because of these rapid fluctuations, medical blood tests to determine hormone function are often inaccurate.

If the pituitary tests weak, test for the corresponding endocrine organ which the pituitary is affecting. A poorly functioning endocrine organ, such as an ovary or a thyroid, will cause the pituitary hormones to increase as the pituitary attempts to stimulate them into functioning properly. Over time, if the condition is not corrected, the pituitary becomes weakened by over exertion. At this point, it is crucial that the health of both the pituitary and the secondary organ be addressed.

A sluggish pituitary gland can often be identified by changes (even subtle changes) in hair growth – scalp, facial, eyebrows, pubic or armpits – because the pituitary directly stimulates the thyroid, adrenals and ovaries to produce thyroxin, adrencorticotropic and estrogen respectively. All of these hormones have a direct effect on hair follicle activity. This can result in fine, dry scalp hair; fine body hair, loss of eyebrow hair, beard hair loss, loss of pubic hair or even small amounts of head hair coming out while washing.

Anterior pituitary gland

1) hGH – human growth hormone (somatotropin) stimulates "insulin like" growth factors that cause cells to multiply by determining the rate at which the cells synthesize protein. In children hGH increases the growth rate of bone and muscle; in adults hGH help maintain muscle and bone mass and promote healing of injuries. Aside from protein synthesis, hGH also affects the breakdown of fat cells (read weight loss) and carbohydrate metabolism (read blood sugar abnormalities). Therefore a deficiency of hGH results in weight gain and increased fat, loss of muscle tissue causing reduced strength and stamina, loss of bone density, poor memory, depression, poor quality sleep, fatigue and reduced quality of life.

Factors that inhibit hGH production include high fat diets, high sugar diets, sluggish thyroid function, obesity, stress, lack of sleep and sleeping in a room which isn't completely dark. hGH is mainly secreted during the night and any light source in the bedroom such as street lights, clock radios, or other night lights will depress the body's production of hGH resulting in a cascade of other hormonal and health problems. Close your curtains and turn off your lights.

Growth hormone production by the pituitary is difficult to evaluate because there is no test that can accurately measure it. Instead, blood tests measure the levels of "insulin like" growth factors which tend to change more slowly in proportion to the overall amount of growth hormone produced by the pituitary.

2) Thyroid stimulating hormone (TSH) stimulates the thyroid to secrete two thyroid hormones: iodothyronine (T3) and thyroxine (T4). A deficiency in TSH can result in weight gain, constipation, dry skin, intolerance to cold, high cholesterol, depression, anxiety, confusion, fatigue and/or poor immunity.

3) Adrenocorticotropic hormone (ACTH) stimulates the production of cortisol, the stress hormone produced by the adrenal glands. Blood sugar disorders, stress and/or physical trauma will increase ACTH production. Deficiency symptoms include: fatigue; low blood pressure; blood sugar imbalances; and an inability to cope with stress.

Production of ACTH is usually measured by assessing the response of cortisol to low blood sugar, induced by an insulin injection. If the level of cortisol doesn't change and the ACTH is normal or low, an ACTH deficiency is confirmed.

4) Follicle stimulating hormone (FSH) is transported to the ovaries where it stimulates follicle and estrogen production in women and testosterone production in men.

5) Luteinizing hormone (LH) is transported to the ovaries and stimulates estrogen, progesterone and testosterone production. It also stimulates the release of the ovary egg during ovulation. A deficiency in either FSH or LH can result in infrequent menstrual periods, infertility, vaginal dryness, testicle atrophy, decreased sperm production and loss of female or male sexual characteristics. FSH and LH can also affect mood swings and energy levels. Because the levels of LH and FSH fluctuate with the menstrual cycle, their measurement in women may be difficult to interpret. In post-menopausal women however, the LH and FSH hormones are normally high, as the pituitary attempts to stimulate estrogen and progesterone production.

6) Prolactin (PRL) initiates and maintains milk secretion by the mammary glands (breasts). It does so by working in conjunction with estrogen, progesterone, hGH, thyroxine and insulin, a fascinating example of how hormones communicate with one another and work together. Prolactin deficiency can cause fatigue, loss of hair, and an inability to produce breast milk.

7) Melanocyte-stimulating hormone (MSH) stimulates the skin to produce melanin, which darkens the skin. MSH increases during pregnancy and adrenal gland disorders such as Addison's and Cushing's Syndromes.

Posterior pituitary gland

1) Oxytocin (OT) is targeted to the uterus during delivery to contract the uterus. After delivery it stimulates breast milk. OT is also controlled by the hypothalamus as is evident when spontaneous milk production occurs after a mother hears her baby cry.

2) Anti-diuretic Hormone (ADH) is a substance that decreases urine production and conserves water and fluids by causing the kidneys to return more water to the blood and by decreasing sweating. Also known as vasopressin, it causes constriction of the blood vessels which increases blood pressure. Production of ADH is controlled by signals from the hypothalamus and is increased by pain, stress, trauma, anxiety, tobacco, and several drugs such as morphine, tranquilizers, and anesthetics. Its production is increased by alcohol…resulting in headaches and hangovers.

Problem Foods – caffeine, sugar, dairy products, wheat, alcohol,
Common Nutrient Deficiencies – iodine, zinc, selenium, vitamin B6 and B12, folic acid
Beneficial Supplements – chaste berry, ginseng, fo-ti, gotu kola, alfalfa

Homeopathic Remedies – pituitary, alfalfa, sepia, ACTH, TSH, FSH

Emotions – The pituitary is the control centre, it is very stable and does not allow itself to become easily disrupted by storing negative emotions, which are more likely to house themselves in the secondary endocrine glands. Ah yes, the wisdom of the body and all its parts…

Advanced Test Points – test each hormone separately – hGH, TSH, FSH, LH, ACTH, MSH, PRL. One hormone or several hormones may be imbalanced.

Supporting Organs – hypothalamus

Pineal

The pineal is a tiny gland located in the centre of the brain between the hemispheres. Although its functions are not clearly understood as yet, we do know that it secretes melatonin, which sets the body's biological clock and induces sleep. Melatonin is derived from the amino acid tryptophan and is mainly secreted when it is dark outside. Melatonin is also a potent antioxidant, protecting the body from free radical damage. While melatonin is the only hormone secreted by the pineal gland, the pineal also contains a number of neurotransmitters such as somatostatin (inhibits growth hormone), serotonin (induces feelings of serenity and optimism) and norepinephrine (elevates mind and mood). The tiny pineal gland is even capable of blocking the master glands: it can keep the hypothalamus from releasing gonadotropin-releasing hormone (GnRH) and the pituitary from releasing the reproductive hormones, LH and FSH. In other words, it seems to have significant control over the sexual/reproductive hormones. René Descartes, the 17th-century French philosopher-mathematician, concluded that the pineal is the "seat of the soul".

Problem Foods – caffeine, sugar, dairy products, wheat, alcohol, excess meat

Common Nutrient Deficiencies – vitamin B6, vitamin C, folic acid, magnesium

Beneficial Supplements – St. John's Wort, alfalfa, fenugreek, fennel

Homeopathic Remedies – pineal, sepia

Emotions – sense of purpose, lack of confidence, guilt

Advanced Test Points – melatonin, specific neurotransmitters

Supporting Organs – brain

Thyroid

The thyroid is a two-lobed butterfly-shaped gland situated just under the larynx. The thyroid combines iodine and tyrosine to produce two major hormones: iodothyronine (T3) and thyroxine (T4). There is four times as much T4 as T3 produced, however T3 is much more potent. These hormones are released into the bloodstream and delivered to every cell in the body, where most of the T4 is converted into T3. These hormones then control the conversion of oxygen and calories from food into energy (ATP), a process commonly known as metabolism. Therefore the thyroid has a major influence on energy levels, basal metabolic rate, and growth and development. It also controls the cellular metabolism of proteins, carbohydrates, fats and nutrients.

Low thyroid function (hypothyroidism) can result in fatigue, muscle weakness or cramps, hip and shoulder pain, weight gain, dry hair, dry skin, hair loss, cold intolerance, constipation, high cholesterol, depression, anxiety, irritability, poor memory, irregular menstrual cycles, low libido, and poor immunity. Repeated various infections and colds and/or flu can be a sign of low thyroid (or low iron levels). In some cases the continuing decline of blood hormone levels causes the pituitary to produce high levels of TSH in an effort to "kick start" the thyroid. If this condition persists it will eventually cause the thyroid to enlarge resulting in a condition known as goiter.

Hair follicles have a high metabolic rate and are thus particularly sensitive to concentrations of thyroid hormones. In all cases of hair loss, check for pituitary and/or thyroid dysfunction as the underlying cause.

The thyroid hormones also enhance the actions of the adrenal hormones (see below). For this reason, symptoms of an over-active thyroid (hyperthyroidism) include increased heart rate, forceful heartbeats, high blood pressure, heat intolerance, frequent bowel movements, tremors, anxiety, agitation, poor concentration, weight loss, insomnia, fatigue and sweating. Hyperthyroidism is often a result of Grave's disease, an auto-immune condition whereby the immune system attacks healthy thyroid tissue causing the thyroid to enlarge and to produce excessive amounts of thyroxine.

Because blood testing hormones can be so unreliable, many holistic practitioners prefer the Barnes Method of thyroid testing, which involves taking the basal body temperature first thing in the morning before getting out of bed. This measures the lowest body temperature of the day. The temperature should be taken under the armpit (axillary) as well as in the mouth (orally) for 4 consecutive days. Normal temperature should be between 36.5 and 36.7 Celsius (97.8 and 98.2 Fahrenheit). If the temperature consistently falls lower than 36.3C (97.4F) then the thyroid can be considered functioning below normal.

The thyroid also produces calcitonin, which lowers blood levels of calcium and phosphates by accelerating the uptake of these minerals into the bone and by inhibiting the breakdown of the bone matrix.

There are also two small round glands attached to the thyroid – these are known as the parathyroid glands. These glands produce parathyroid hormone (PTH) that acts to control calcium levels in the blood. When blood calcium is too low PTH is secreted and causes calcium to be released from storage depots - bone and muscles - back into the blood. When the blood calcium is too high, less PTH is released, allowing calcium levels to drop again. PTH also increases dietary absorption of calcium by activating vitamin D (calcitrol) and conserves calcium by causing the kidneys to reabsorb calcium. In the same way, PTH also regulates magnesium levels. As well, PTH decreases phosphates by causing more excretion through the kidneys.

Because calcium is alkaline and phosphates are acidic, a healthy thyroid is a key player in maintaining a healthy PH balance in the blood by adjusting the absorption, release and excretion of minerals and acids.

Problem Foods – caffeine, sugar, dairy products, wheat, high carbohydrate diets
Common Nutrient Deficiencies – iodine, selenium, calcium, Vitamin B6, folic acid, tyrosine,
Beneficial Supplements – kelp, Oregon grape root, ashwaghanda, lemon balm, creatinine monohydrate
Homeopathic Remedies – thyroid, TSH, sepia, calc carb, iodine
Emotions – stubbornness, depression, anxiety, lack of nurturing
Advanced Test Points – T3, T4, parathyroids
Supporting organs – pituitary, adrenals, pancreas (insulin), ovaries, testes

Adrenals

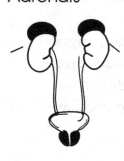

Small but powerful one adrenal gland lies on top of each kidney. Each adrenal gland consists of an outer layer, the adrenal cortex, and the inner core known as the adrenal medulla. Despite their small size (about the size of your thumb) the adrenal glands may play the most significant role of any of the organs in combating stress. During episodes of chronic stress such as fatigue, physical illness, anxiety and/or depression, these glands - just like the thymus - will actually shrink.

Adrenal Cortex
The cortex secretes three different types of hormones, all of which are essential to life. They are all steroid hormones that use cho-

lesterol as their starting material. And all of them are triggered by the release of ACTH from the pituitary.

1) Mineralcorticoids
As the name suggests, mineralcorticoids affect mineral balance by controlling water flow. The main mineral corticoid hormone is aldosterone, "the salt hormone" which acts on the kidneys to promote re-absorption of salt into the blood. Through the process of osmosis, water follows the salt thus affecting the maintenance of blood pressure. Aldosterone also controls the amount of salt that the sweat glands secrete when perspiring and increases the sensitivity of taste buds to sodium. Aldosterone secretion is stimulated by low salt levels, high potassium levels, and secretion of angiotensin II, a blood pressure hormone released by the kidneys.

2) Glucocorticoids
The main hormone in this group is cortisone. Cortisone stimulates the breakdown (catabolism) of both fats and proteins; it converts proteins or lactic acids into sugars which then flood the blood system, providing a ready source of energy during "fight or flight" episodes. Therefore, cortisone production is maximized during all episodes of stress, including exercise, fasting, diabetic episodes, disease, bleeding, trauma, injury and intense emotions such as fear and anger. Cortisone also acts as a natural anti-inflammatory for pain and inflammation.

Chronically high levels of cortisone induced by stress or through cortisone medications (as is popular with arthritis or other chronic pain conditions) depresses the immune response, resulting in a variety of other health problems including lowering resistance to infection. In fact, cortisone is such an effective immune suppressant that it is used as an immunosuppressive drug after organ transplants. High cortisone levels will also delay healing by discouraging the formation of new connective tissue and wound healing. Avoid high sugar diets, long periods of stress and/or long-term courses of steroid medications.

3) Androgens

This class of hormones is male sex hormones with the main one being a precursor to testosterone, DHEA (dehydroepiandrosterone). While both men and women produce DHEA through the adrenal glands, men produce most of it through the testicles with only a small amount produced by the adrenals. Women, on the other hand, produce the majority of DHEA through the adrenals, which then convert the DHEA to either testosterone or estrogen. Testosterone contributes to libido and body hair growth including pubic and armpits. DHEA is converted into estrogen during menopause when the ovarian secretion of estrogens stops. For this reason adrenal health is very important during peri-menopause and menopause.

Adrenal Medulla

 1) The principal hormone synthesized by the medulla is adrenaline (epinephrine). Smaller amounts of noradrenalin (norepinephrine) are also produced. These hormones prepare us for "fight or flight" mode by increasing heart rate, heart force and pumping output. This increases blood pressure and blood flow to the heart, liver, muscles and fat tissue. Adrenaline also dilates the airways to the lungs and increases blood sugar and blood fats. In stressful situations and during exercise, the hypothalamus releases acetylcholine, a brain neurotransmitter, that causes an increase in adrenaline.

Problem Foods – caffeine, sugar, glutens
Common Nutrient Deficiencies – iodine, evening primrose oil, vitamin B5, vitamin C, magnesium, calcium
Beneficial Supplements – kelp, licorice root, ginseng, ashwaghanda, yucca, chamomile
Homeopathic Remedies – hypothalamus, adrenal, adrenaline, phosphorus, sepia, chamomila
Emotions – fear, impatience, anger
Advanced Test Points – aldosterone, cortisone, testosterone, adrenaline
Supporting Organs – hypothalamus, pituitary

More About Stress

Everyday living is a stressor. The seemingly simple acts of feeding ourselves, housing ourselves, providing for ourselves and being in relationship with one another cause regular stresses of different levels. It is therefore impossible to remove all stress from our lives. Some stress, called eustress is actually positive stress, such as exciting and fun events that prepare us to meet life's challenges with increased vitality. Eustress contributes to our health and happiness and improves the immune system. Conversely, negative stress or distress is uncomfortable and is almost always harmful, eventually leading to major health challenges. If exposure to a stressor is prolonged, the stress response occurs in three stages:

a) **The alarm reaction** - fight or flight response - initiated by the hypothalamus. Large amounts of sugar, blood and oxygen are delivered by increased circulation to the organs in danger: the brain becomes more alert, the muscles strengthen and the heart pumps harder. The digestive, urinary and reproductive systems are considered non-essential and are therefore inhibited.

b) **The resistance reaction** is a longer term reaction whereby the pituitary releases human growth hormones (hGH), TSH to promote thyroid hormones and ACTH to stimulate more adrenal production of cortisol. The end result is an increase in cellular energy (ATP), enzymes and circulatory changes to enable us to meet emotional crises and perform strenuous tasks.

c) **The exhaustion stage** occurs when the resistance stage cannot be sustained. At this point all of the hormone changes as discussed can cause muscle wasting, immune suppression, digestive problems, low sex drive, headaches, diabetes, heart problems, high blood pressure, anxiety, depression and any other problems that we are particularly prone to as individuals. Stress normally affects those body systems that

are already weak and deficient. The exhaustion stage is often termed "adrenal burn-out" and the adrenals will require attention, treatment and support even after the stressor has finally been removed. Adrenal burn-out is the reason that physical and emotional symptoms can continue to persist for a long period of time after the stressful episodes are over.

Stress levels are determined by our response, not by the event

Ovaries

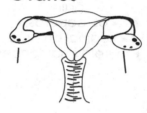

The ovaries are a pair of reproductive glands situated on either side of the uterus. Each ovary is about the size and shape of an almond. The ovaries produce both estrogen and progesterone, which are actually steroids. They regulate the menstrual cycle, maintain pregnancy and prepare the breasts for breast-feeding. They also control the development of female body characteristics – breasts, uterus, body shape and hair, as well as an increase in fat tissue. Estrogen plays a role in maintaining bone density and in blood clotting.

Both estrogen and progesterone have a profound effect on brain function: estrogen has an excitatory effect on the brain, increasing serotonin and acetylcholine levels whereas progesterone has a more calming effect. Serotonin is responsible for creating positive moods and acetylcholine is necessary for a healthy memory. Thus many women with hormonal imbalances report mood swings, poor memory and other mental and emotional difficulties. Hormones are powerful chemicals with minor fluctuations capable of producing disturbing symptoms.

EXCESS ESTROGEN SYMPTOMS	DEFICIENT ESTROGEN SYMPTOMS
• Fibrocysts	• fatigue
• abdominal weight gain	• hot flashes
• water retention	• chocolate cravings
• depression	• memory lapses
• anxiety headaches and migraines	• dry skin
• insomnia	• low sex drive
• blood clots	• anxiety
• diabetes	• abdominal weight gain
• sluggish metabolism	• osteoporosis
• low sex drive	• vaginal dryness
• PMS	• thyroid imbalances
• ovarian cysts	
• heavy menstrual bleeding and prolonged periods	
• breast tenderness	
• breast cancer	
• uterine cancer	
• ovarian cancer	
• immune disorders	

EXCESS PROGESTERONE SYMPTOMS	DEFICIENT PROGESTERONE SYMPTOMS
• fatigue	• infertility
• depressions	• depression
• digestive problems	• weight gain
	• low blood sugar
	• dry skin
	• vaginal dryness
	• join pain

Estrogen imbalances are mainly a result of diets high in sugar, carbohydrates, dairy products, beef and caffeine. As well, many of our commercial meats contain estrogen-like growth hormones. Once the estrogen levels increase, the body will almost always gain weight. The increase in fat cells results in higher estrogen production which then creates more weight gain and the treadmill begins. In cases of estrogen deficiency, the body will also begin to gain weight, especially abdominal weight since abdominal fat cells will produce more estrogen. The instinctual wisdom of the body chemistry considers the deficiency of estrogen more detrimental than extra pounds. Thus, in the case of either a deficiency or excess of estrogen the body will begin to crave more food, particularly carbohydrates, which it cannot now efficiently metabolize since estrogen imbalances also alter the metabolism. And then stress plays its role by depressing adrenal function, which decreases progesterone levels resulting in higher estrogen levels.

Menopausal and peri-menopausal women are particularly at risk. A woman's body during menopause senses that her child-bearing years are coming to a close, so the reproductive system produces increasingly high levels of estrogen to try and encourage reproduction (just in case you change your mind). Or, the natural process of aging will simply begin to decrease hormone levels. Unfortunately, modern diets, caffeine, excess body weight, stress levels and medical attitudes have transformed women's health into a 20th century disease. Life's transitions - puberty, pregnancy or menopause – have been a natural part of women's lives since the beginning of time. In a healthy body these transitions should be celebrated, not "drugged".

Problem Foods – caffeine, dairy products, beef, sugar, high carbohydrates

Common Nutrient Deficiencies – iodine, vitamin B6, vitamin E, folic acid, magnesium, phosphorus

Beneficial Supplements – evening primrose oil, kelp, dang quai, wild yam, licorice root, black cohosh, blue cohosh, royal jelly, phosphatidyl choline

Homeopathic Remedies – ovarinum, lachesis, pulsatilla, sepia, sulphur, caulophyllum phosphorus

Emotions – depression and anger - especially as a result of abuse, poor body image, inability to enjoy sex, staying in unhappy relationships

Advanced Test Points – estrogen, progesterone

Supporting Organs – pituitary, thyroid, adrenals

Testes

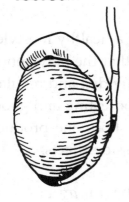

Men have two testes that produce dehydroepi-androsterone (DHEA), which is a precursor to the steroid hormone testosterone, the primary androgen. Testosterone regulates the production of sperm and stimulates the development of masculine sex characteristics such as body and facial hair, muscle mass and strength, as well as bone mass. Similar to estrogen, testosterone also has an effect on brain neurotransmitters, particularly dopamine. Although testosterone levels begin to decrease after the age of forty, the most common causes for hormonal decrease

are dietary habits, excess weight, diabetes, caffeine consumption, smoking, excess alcohol consumption and stress.

Problem Foods – caffeine, dairy products, sugar, high fat, low fibre

Common Nutrient Deficiencies – iodine, vitamin B6, vitamin E, folic acid, magnesium, zinc

Beneficial Supplements – evening primrose oil, kelp, ginseng, puncture vine, horny goat weed

Homeopathic Remedies – testes

Emotions – anger, aggression, feelings of inferiority

Advanced test points – testosterone

Supporting organs – pituitary, adrenals, prostate

> **LOW TESTOSTERONE LEVELS CAN CAUSE A VARIETY OF PROBLEMS FOR MEN, INCLUDING:**
> - fatigue
> - depression
> - mood swings
> - irritability
> - aggression
> - impotence
> - inability to orgasm
> - poor mental concentration
> - loss of muscle strength
> - abdominal weight gain
> - insomnia
> - diabetes
> - cardiovascular diseases

Aging and the Endocrine System

Although some endocrine glands shrink as we get older, resulting in lowered hormone levels, some hormone levels actually increase.

HORMONES THAT DECREASE:
- human Growth Hormone (hGH) - causing muscle weakness and wasting
- Thyroxine - causing a drop in metabolic rate
- Cortisol - causing lowered immunity and stress responses
- Aldosterone - causing changes in blood pressure
- Insulin - resulting in higher blood sugar levels
- Estrogen - increasing the risk for osteoporosis and hardening of the arteries
- Testosterone - causing lower sperm counts and lowered libido

- -

HORMONES THAT INCREASE
- Follicle stimulating hormone (FSH) - increases to stimulate ovary hormone production**
- Luteinizing hormone (LH) - increases to stimulate ovary hormone production**
- Thyroid stimulating hormone (TSH) - works to increase thyroid output**
- Testosterone in women - results in an increase in confidence and self-worth

**It is therefore important to support pituitary and thyroid function during hormone transitions.

- -

HORMONES THAT REMAIN UNCHANGED
- adenocorticotropic hormone (ACTH)
- adrenaline

Hormone Supplementation

It has become popular in both modern medicine and natural health to supplement with hormones as a panacea for everything that ails us. It is my opinion that hormonal supplementation – whether pharmaceutical, natural or bio-identical plant hormones - should be avoided as much as possible. Hormones are very powerful chemicals over which the human body has remarkable control. They are naturally secreted by the various glands in very minute but exact doses with exact timing. It is a complex system of inter-communication and feedback from one endocrine gland to another and from one hormone to another. This organization is not only very difficult to mimic artificially but an imbalance in one hormone always throws out the balance of at least one other hormone.

Side effects prevail – here are some examples:
- Hormone Replacement Therapy of estrogen and progesterone has been linked to an increase in heart disease, strokes, lung and leg blood clots, breast cancer, uterine cancer and dementia.
- Melatonin in several animal species has caused atrophy (wasting away) of ovaries and testicles.
- DHEA is synthesized in the lab from soy and wild yam and can cause hair loss, acne, lowered voice, facial hair, mood swings and reproductive cancers.
- hGH can cause joint pain, abnormal bone thickening, increased blood pressure, and insulin resistance.

There is no substitute for a healthy lifestyle. Study after study shows that the only genuine youth elixir is a healthy diet and regular exercise. Good living, good eating and good thinking increase healthy hormone production and a host of positive side effects.

There will never be a magical panacea for youth – other than joyful living

Brain

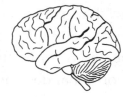

The human brain is an amazing and fascinating 1-1/2 kg organ that acts as a control centre to receive, interpret and direct sensory information throughout the body. It receives multiple messages through our five senses: sight; smell; hearing; touch and taste. The forebrain (frontal lobe) is responsible for receiving and processing this information as well as thinking, perceiving and understanding language and motor function. The midbrain conducts auditory and visual responses, while the hindbrain allows us to maintain balance, equilibrium and coordination, as well as controlling the autonomic functions of breathing, heart rate and digestion. The brain is protected by thick skull bones and cerebrospinal fluid and is isolated from the general bloodstream by the blood-brain barrier.

The brain and its neurotransmitters are extremely sensitive. Neurotransmitters are chemicals that transmit and relay messages from one nerve cell (neuron) to another. This is how the neurons communicate with one another. There are over 50 neurotransmitters identified, however the common ones include acetylcholine and norepinephrine (excitatory) and dopamine, serotonin and gamma aminobutyric acid (GABA) which are inhibitory. Each neurotransmitter directly influences the action of the neurons in specific areas of the brain, thereby affecting behaviour and mental disorders such as depression, anxiety, attention deficits, hyperactivity, addictions, dementia, Alzheimer's and personality disorders. We often forget that the brain too is a specialized organ that requires healthy food and nutrition for optimum function. It is very sensitive to the effects of food allergies as well as nutrient deficiencies. Food and nutrition alters memory, learning abilities, mo-

tor control, speech, focus, behavioural abnormalities, and moods.

Problem Foods – caffeine, sugar, dairy products, wheat, glutens, meat, preservatives, artificial flavours and colourings
Common Nutrient Deficiencies –vitamins B6 and B12, folic acid, iron, zinc, magnesium
Beneficial Supplements – phosphatidyl choline, phosphatidyl serine, lecithin, evening primrose oil, fish oils, gotu kola, foti, gingko biloba, ginseng, ashwaghanda
Homeopathic Remedies – hypothalamus, phosphorus, phosphoric acid
Emotions to test –there is not one emotion that does not have a powerful impact on brain chemistry – see page 100
Advanced Test Points – specific neurotransmitters – acetylcholine, norepinephrine, dopamine, serotonin, GABA
Supporting Organs – hypothalamus

Skin

The skin is the largest organ of the body, whose function is to protect the body and to regulate body temperature. It consists of 3 layers: the dermis; epidermis (containing hair follicles and sweat glands) and hypodermis (made of fat and connective tissue). Skin colour is created by melanocytes which produce the pigment melanin.

Along with the kidneys, liver, lungs and colon, the skin is a major elimination organ, helping to rid the body of toxins accumulated from air, water, food, digestive metabolism, bacteria, viruses, parasites, dead cells and stress. External toxins include heavy metals, chemicals, molds and pesticides. Both external and internal toxins can affect metabolism, immunity, hormones, brain chemistry, arteries, and the heart.

The skin can sweat off up to one kilogram of toxic waste daily and it produces a new layer of skin every 24 hours. Perspiration (sweat) contains water, salt, urea (produced by meat eating) and pheromones (chemicals secreted by humans, animals and insects that influence the behaviour of the same species, particularly as an attraction to the opposite sex). And even though sweating is unable to eliminate all toxins, it does act to increase blood and lymphatic circulation, thus encouraging the other elimination organs to detoxify more efficiently. And so, even though the kidneys, liver and lungs eliminate much more waste than the skin, when these organs become congested, the skin must handle the overload. It is at these times that we start to see a variety of skin conditions: eczema, dermatitis, psoriasis, acne, hives, rashes, and eruptions.

The skin has a protective layer known as the acid mantle, a layer of lactic acid that protects the skin from bacteria, parasites, insects and infections. Like any organ of the body, the acid mantle can be damaged by diet, poor nutrition, stress, poor immunity, blood toxins and food allergies. It then loses acidity (higher pH) which predisposes the skin to inflammation, infection and hypersensitivities. If the acid mantle layer has been disrupted you will attract far more insect bites than someone with a healthy acid mantle, and suffer from more skin allergy reactions as well as skin infections.

Problem Foods – fats and oils, dairy products, sugar, wheat, citrus fruit, tomatoes

Common Nutrient Deficiencies – vitamin B6, vitamin C, calcium, iron, iodine, selenium, silica, sulphur

Beneficial Supplements – yellow dock, chickweed, plantain, calendula, milk thistle, flax seed, evening primrose oil, vinegar

External Remedies – tea tree oil, calendula, chickweed, coconut oil, vinegar, zinc ointment

Homeopathic Remedies – sulphur, calcarea carb, graphites, silicea, arsenicum, kali sulph, psorinum

Emotions – feeling defenseless, suppressed anger, suppression of personal needs

Advanced Test Points – yeast, bacteria

Supporting organs – large colon, liver, lymph, blood

Bones and Teeth

 Bone is a specialized form of connective tissue. It is composed of collagen - a tough, fibrous protein - proteins, sugar based polysaccharides known as glycans, and a variety of minerals that serve to strengthen bone density. In compact bone, the hard outer layer of bone, the mineralized mixture is full of small channels (Haversian canals) that contain blood vessels and nerves. The spongy, or cancellous, part of the bone is

a honeycomb structure and typically occurs at the ends of long bones, next to the joints and inside the vertebrae. It is much softer and weaker than compact bone, allowing for more flexibility. It is highly vascular and contains red bone marrow. Red bone marrow is also found in the flat bones – hip, breast, skull, shoulder blades and vertebrae. Red bone marrow produces and releases millions of red blood cells (erythrocytes) that function to carry oxygen throughout the body as well as to collect carbon dioxide. Red bone marrow is also an important part of the lymph and immune system as it produces millions of white blood cells (leukocytes) to defend the body against infections and foreign invaders. With age, the bones also serve to store fat cells (adipose) as yellow marrow found in the centre of the long bones. An excess of yellow marrow will affect both red blood cell production and immunity.

Bones are living, growing tissue and during a lifetime, it is constantly being renewed. Old bone is removed and new bone is laid down in a process of bone remodeling that strengthens and increases density and allows for the repair of micro-fractures. The entire skeleton is capable of replacing itself every 10 years. Before new bone can form, cells called osteoclasts dissolve some tissue on the bone's surface, creating a small cavity (re-sorption). Then cells called osteoblasts fill the cavities with collagen (formation) which hardens with deposits of minerals – calcium and phosphorus as well as the trace minerals zinc, silica, boron, sulphur, manganese and vanadium. The bone also acts as a storage tissue for minerals, releasing them back into the blood as required.

While it is important to correct existing mineral deficiencies it is also important to avoid excessive supplementation as the bones will be unable to store the excess. When in excess, minerals are released into the blood where they can cause a variety of problems. Interestingly enough, symptoms of mineral deficiencies (as well as vitamin deficiencies) are often the same as the symptoms of excess.

In good health, bone formation and bone re-sorption occur at equal rates. However, when the rate of re-sorption exceeds the rate of formation, bone density and quality of bone decrease and the bone becomes very porous and weakens. This imbalance predisposes us to a variety of bone diseases including osteoporosis (porous bones), osteopenia (low bone minerals), osteoarthritis (degeneration of bone cartilage), and osteomyelitis (infection). Factors that negatively affect the remodeling process are high acid diets, high sugar diets, caffeine, cigarette smoking, steroids, drugs, hormonal imbalances, nutrient deficiencies and a lack of weight-bearing exercise.

Tooth enamel is the hardest and most highly mineralized substance in the body. The high mineral content gives it incredible strength and hardness. Cavities are caused by bacteria which feed on refined carbohydrates. The bacteria then produce acids which begin to dissolve tooth enamel, resulting in cavities. Poor diets and faulty nutrition are related to cavities, gum diseases, crooked teeth and other tooth abnormalities.

One of the biggest causes of bone and dental disease is the destructive effect of high dietary acids from food or water. These acids will increase the re-sorption process and degenerate and damage bone, joint and tooth tissue. It is too often assumed that common bone diseases such as osteoporosis and osteoarthritis are necessary challenges of aging. They are not! High acid levels can be prevented and treated through diet, exercise, appropriate nutritional supplements and alkaline water. Excess acid levels also affect the integrity of minerals. Calcium and phosphorus form a mineral complex known as hydroxyapatite giving bones and teeth a tremendous amount of strength. However, when hydroxyapatite is combined with water and acids it forms crystals of hydroxyapatite which deposit themselves in and around the joints, causing inflammation and pain leading to arthritis and other degenerative bone diseases. These crystals also contribute to dental cavities.

Problem Foods – sugar, refined carbohydrates, vinegar, citrus fruit, all fruit, potatoes, beef
Common Nutrient Deficiencies – vitamins C, D and A, Coenzyme Q10, silica, sulphur, iron, calcium, magnesium
Beneficial Supplements – alkaline water,
Homeopathic Remedies – arnica, rhus-tox, ruta grav, sulphur, symphytum
Emotions – bones – rigid thinking, secrets ("skeletons in the closet") arthritis – lack of flexibility, frustration, resentment
Advanced Test Points – red blood cells, white blood cells, bacteria, yeast, viruses
Supporting Organs – liver, blood

Muscles and Connective Tissue

 There are three different types of major muscle. Smooth muscle tissue is located in the walls of hollow internal structures - blood vessels, stomach, intestines and urinary bladder. Smooth muscle fibers are involuntary and are not under our conscious control. Skeletal muscle tissue is striated and is always attached to the bones. Skeletal muscle tissue is under conscious control and can be made to contract or relax voluntarily. Cardiac muscle tissue forms the heart wall. Like skeletal muscle tissue it is striated, however the contraction is not under conscious control.

Skeletal muscles are composed of two different types of fibre: Type I fibres are known as "slow-twitch" fibres: dark in colour, loaded with mitochondria, resistant to fatigue, and reliant on oxygen for energy production (ATP). Volatile fatty acids (from glycogen, sugar and fat) are the major energy source in "slow-twitch" fibres – these fibres are dominant in endurance muscles and would therefore be predominant in a long-distance runner or a tri-athlete, for example.

Type II fibres are "fast twitch" fibres: white in colour, few mitochondria, anaerobic (i.e. do not use oxygen for energy production), depend on glycolysis for energy and fatigue easily with the production of lactic acid. Glycolysis is the process of glycogen or sugar converting into energy (ATP) without oxygen. Excess sugar is converted into glycogen, which is a form of starch stored in the liver and muscles for future use. "Fast-twitch" fibres are used for rapid movement such as eyeball muscles and are more dominant in people such as sprinters, who do quick speed events. "Fast twitch" fibres are only able to perform for short periods of time.

If excess muscle performance requires energy production faster than our bodies can adequately deliver oxygen, or if the muscles are unable to utilize adequate amounts of oxygen, they are forced to go into glycolysis which produces lactic acid. When lactic acid (or dietary acids for that matter) are accumulated faster than they can be metabolized it becomes the primary cause of muscle fatigue, pain and stiffness. When the muscles of an endurance athlete fatigue it is the result of glycogen depletion (no fuel) rather than a build up of excess lactic acid. Lactic acid build up is caused by poor conditioning, slow metabolism, poor cardiovascular fitness, lack of exercise, and toxicity due to waste products. Diets high in sugar, excess protein (meat) and acids, largely contribute to muscle problems. Many so-called age-related aches and pains are nothing more than high acid and toxic diets combined with a lack of movement.

Connective tissue is found throughout the body and binds together and connects structures of the body. It supports other tissues and organs and includes various kinds of fibrous tissue, fat, bone, cartilage, tendons and ligaments. Tendons attach muscles to bone and ligaments attach bone to bone. Tendons and ligaments have poor blood supply and can therefore take more time to heal than do other tissues.

Problem Foods – sugar, beef, potatoes, citrus fruit, all fruit, vinegar
Common Nutrient Deficiencies – sulphur, magnesium, calcium, iron, selenium, potassium, vitamin E, dimethylglycine (DMG)
Beneficial Supplements – hyaluronic acid, methylsulfonylmethane (MSM), creatinine monohydrate
Homeopathic Remedies – arnica, bryonia, rhus-tox, ruta grav, sulphur, mag phos, sarco-lactic acid
Emotions – resentment, control
Advanced Test Points – muscles, tendons, ligaments, skeletal muscle, smooth muscle, cardiac muscle
Supporting Organs – colon, liver, blood

Other Important Test Points

Protein Levels
The body always requires adequate protein levels. Protein deficiencies (or excess) can cause changes to growth rates in children, bone and muscle function (including muscle shrinkage), energy levels, immunity, body weight, liver function, and fluid retention. To test protein levels hold a piece of head hair while testing. A weak response indicates protein imbalance; a neutral or strong response indicates balance. To determine whether or not the protein levels are low or high, test the muscle response by holding the hair with *your palm facing up*: a weak response indicates high protein levels. Then hold a piece of hair with *your palm facing down*: a weak response indicates low protein levels. Do not test a high or low response unless the general protein point is unbalanced.

Fat Status

To test the fat condition of the body, find an area on the body with fat tissue, usually the abdomen, buttocks, thighs or breasts. Access the fat with one hand while testing with the other. If there is an imbalance (a weak response) then further test for which dietary fats are potentially causing problems. Test any fats that the person may be ingesting, including the ones hidden in processed or baked foods. Include meat fat, trans-fats, hydrogenated oils, deep-fried fats, margarine, butter, mayonnaise, vegetable oils, corn oil, safflower oil, coconut oil, soya oil, canola oil, olive oil, etc. In addition, test for the health benefits of "good" fats: evening primrose oil; fish oil; lecithin; phosphatidyl choline; flax seeds and hemp seeds.

Technique Reminders for Body Testing (See Chapter 5)

1) Touch the organ point with your fingers or part of your hand while checking the person's muscle response. A weak muscle response indicates an imbalance in that particular organ meridian. A strong or neutral muscle response indicates no imbalances for that organ at that particular time.

2) To test the effect of food on any particular organ, hold it against the point itself. A weak muscle response indicates that the food is a problem and is causing symptoms.

3) To determine nutrient deficiencies, have the client close their eyes while you slowly and methodically verbally call out each vitamin and mineral by name. A weak muscle response indicates there is an imbalance – usually a deficiency – unless the client is already taking the nutrient, which often indicates that it is in excess. Be sure to ask!

However, since the common nutrient deficiencies are listed in this chapter you may also test the nutrients by directly holding them against the point. Once again, a weak response indicates that the nutrient should not be supplemented whereas a strong response indicates that the nutrient can be taken with benefit.

4) To test the effect of any nutrient, supplement, or homeopathic remedy on a particular organ, have the client hold the item against the point. If you don't have the actual supplement or remedy with you, have both you and the client close your eyes and visualize the item. For added focus, say it out loud. A weak muscle response indicates that the supplement is of no benefit and may even be aggravating the condition. A strong muscle response indicates that the supplement is of benefit.

Emotional Kinesiology

As discussed, every part of the body is capable of storing emotions as a result of trauma. The physical storage of emotion starts as a "thought form" (an energy field) which we create by our emotional reaction to our interactions with the world around us. If the impact of the event is more than we can consciously process within the framework of a healthy emotional response, then the event causes a form of emotional paralysis. The shocked emotions perpetrated by the event then seek refuge in the physical body, and become a "shadow". The physical body is a dense and relatively "heavy" vibration that embraces, stores and lovingly protects these emotions. The body can only handle so much, and with time, these repressed emotions begin to disrupt and disorganize the harmonious frequency of light and information that assemble the body. We manifest this disruption as physical discomfort and disease.

If the events continue to repeat themselves, the "thought forms" become belief systems - which are almost always false – but even so they then form our patterns of consciousness and the windows through which we perceive the world. The sequence is as follows: we experience a negative event which causes emotional pain; we store it in our memory as well as somewhere in the body; then we form a belief system to justify the experience; then we validate this belief system through repetitive behaviour; and then finally the process becomes a pattern which only serves to attract more of the same. Whew! No wonder we become so exhausted.

For example, let's say that your father and mother separated when you were 4 years old and your father drifted off permanently leaving you feeling lost, unloved and abandoned. Then at age 18 your first serious boyfriend or girlfriend (the one you thought you were going to marry) decided that the relationship was not what they wanted after all – once again leaving you feeling lost, unloved and abandoned except this time it's more painful. Both times you store these painful emotions in the lungs and lower back. Now sub-consciously - and perhaps consciously as well – you conclude that you are not worthy of anyone's love or attention which explains why people like to abandon you. This now becomes your belief system so your psyche begins to choose events and people, including family, friends and lovers that are most likely to emotionally hurt you. At this point you will feel compelled to play the "blame game" not realizing that the pattern that you have just created is manifested by your own belief systems.

While these patterns are often formed by our life experiences, they are also determined by the nature and history of our soul, meaning that we can be, and usually are, born with multiple patterns and emotional storage depots. Core wounds such as abandonment, rejection, inability to love or to be loved, insecurity, blame, anger, resentment, the need to control or to be perfect, religious miasms, shame and grief are all examples of major emotional themes that we may be born with and/or produce in one life time. It is my experience however, that most core wounds are buried deep in the soul's shadow world and that the pattern keeps on perpetuating itself time after time over several soul experiences, including this one, until the pattern is broken through self-awareness and soul retrieval.

Interestingly enough, environmental influences such as diet, nutrition, bacteria, viruses and pollutants act as "triggers", weakening those areas of the body that are already burdened or stressed by emotional and cellular memory. This is why a particular food allergy or a cold virus, for example, can be prolonged or develop into other physical or emotional symptoms. It also explains why the same "flu bug" will affect different people in a variety of different ways: the reaction is body-unique for each person.

Physical accidents and traumas are either re-creations of core wounds (attracting the same pattern of pain or punishment) or an attempt by the body to alleviate the pressure. Body trauma is also used to get attention.

While in-depth emotional therapy is beyond the scope of this book, we can make profound changes by identifying and bringing to light the variety of emotions, patterns and layers which we had not yet been made aware of. Once again, the simple act of observation and shedding light upon the shadow can initiate a deep healing by shifting the energy enough to release the memory. Once the memory has been released, the emotional pain goes with it. The added benefit is that this is often accomplished without any trauma drama, a common response to other psychotherapeutic modalities.

Step 1 - Identifying the Problem

Using these columns of listed emotions and issues you will keep one hand on the affected body part while verbally naming the emotions. To save time, test an entire column separately first – a weak response indicates that the emotion you are looking for is listed within that column. Then verbally call out each emotion in the column. When the muscle strength weakens, it indicates that this emotion is distressing and needs attention. Remember, you are not asking the body any

LIST OF COMMON EMOTIONS

Abandonment	Disappointment	Intolerance	Repression
Abuse	Discouragement	Insecurity	Resentment
Addiction	Dishonesty	Irritability	Resistance
Acceptance	Disorientation		Responsibility
Aggressiveness	Distrust	Judgement	Revenge
Alcoholism	Domineering	Laziness	
Anger	Doubt	Loneliness	Sadism
Anxiety	Drugs	Love	Sadness
Apathy		Martyrdom	Secrecy
Attachment	Ego	Masochism	Selfishness
Attention	Envy	Materialism	Self-esteem
	Failure	Morality	Self-image
Betrayal	Faith	Negativity	Self-punishment
Bitterness	Fear	Non-attachment	Self-worth
Blame	Forgiveness		Sentimental
Boredom	Frustration	Obsession	Separation
Brain trauma	Greed	Oversensitivity	Sexual distress
Complaining	Grief	Overwhelm	Shock
Confidence	Guilt	Panic	Sympathy
Control		Paranoia	Shame
Courage	Habit Patterns	Perfectionism	Stubbornness
Criticism	Hatred of self	Pessimism	
Cruelty	Hatred of others	Possessiveness	Terror
	Hopelessness	Power	Trauma
Defensiveness	Impatience	Prejudice	Violence
Defiance	Inadequacy	Pride	Vulnerability
Denial	Injustice		
Depression	Inner Child	Rebelliousness	
Despair	Intimacy	Religion	

110

questions; you are testing the resonance between the body system and the emotion. Let the body do the talking.

Quite often the person immediately recalls the event and/or the response once the emotion is heard or felt and no further action is required aside from compassionate presence. However, if more information is required to determine the underlying event, move on to Step 2.

Step 2 – Identifying the Relationship
Most traumatic events and emotions have their beginnings in our interaction with other people. It is therefore beneficial to acknowledge the relationship that is causing us distress at any specific time. This is not for confrontation purposes but to simply give us awareness as to where we need to focus our healing energy. Identify the relationship by verbally naming each title and waiting for a weak muscle response, which indicates a dissonant relationship.

Step 3 – Identifying the Time and Place
Information about time and location can also help us bring our issues to light. The added information of when and where our traumas took place helps our sub-conscious to "let go" and "release". A weak muscle response indicates that this particular time/dimension is troubling. (Note that "alternate life" pertains to what most readers will know as a "past life". I avoid the term past life since the past is not possible: a linear time line does not exist in the universal soul; the soul is capable of having multiple experiences simultaneously. Think of your soul's evolution as being synchronous or circular rather than linear.

The emotional kinesiology tables are also found in the Appendix.

LIST OF RELATIONSHIPS	
Wife	Teacher
Husband	Leader
Ex-wife	Mentor
Ex-husband	Family group
Mother	
Father	
Son	Higher self
Daughter	Higher guide
Brother	Angel
Sister	Discarnate
Uncle	Religious group
Aunt	Church
Grandfather	Other groups
Grandmother	Supreme Being such as God
Friend	(or any deity worshiped)
Neighbour	
Business Associate	
Co-Worker	

TIMELINE	
Alternate/other life	
Parallel universe	
Death	
Bardo	
Current event	
Future event	
Past event	- Conception
	- Birth
	- Womb
	- Infant
	- Childhood to age 12
	- Teenager
	- Age 20's
	- Age 30's
	- Age 40's
	- Age 50's
	- Age 60's
	- Age 70's
	- Age 80's
- If you're older than 90 congratulations you don't need to be reading this book, you need to be writing it.	

Is There More?

In this chapter, we focused on the individual body parts and systems to learn about their specific functions, what imbalances can occur, and how to identify, prevent, treat and correct them using **The Marijke Method**™. In Chapter 7 we will learn how to test for the appropriate diet and cleansing programs. Enjoy…

Chapter 7

TESTING DIET and CLEANSING PROGRAMS
-Listen to Your Body-

As we have seen in the previous chapters, the impact of food and nutrition on health and disease is significant. Diet is the single most important therapy in determining the outcome of your healing journey. Rather than the confusion of riding the merry-go-around of endless possible diet programs, you will now - with your skills in kinesiology - be able to establish the correct therapeutic diet for any specific stage in your healing. This ability will bless you with remarkable results...

Trust your body

The following diet plans can be energy tested by number. To save time, energy test them in groups. For example, test group numbers 1 to 5, 6 to 10, 11 to 15, 16 to 19 and 21 to 25. Once it is determined which group gives the strongest muscle response (i.e. the most beneficial) then each number in that group can be tested separately. It is not necessary to know or to memorize which diet belongs to each number. In fact, it is often better not to know.

If more than one diet plan tests strongly, then re-test to find out which diet plan should be started first. Any other programs can be re-tested later. Use the food list in the Appendix to make an easy-to-follow plan for your food program.

While it is important to stick to any program as best you can for maximum benefit, it is equally important that you not let yourself become fanatical. There is no need for your eating habits to become extreme. Always seek balance – physically, mentally, emotionally and spiritually.

With any diet program or cleanse test for nutrient deficiencies regularly - especially for long-term programs, more restrictive programs and for cleanses.

Trust the Wisdom of the Body

List Of Diets

1) Paleolithic (Caveman and Cavewoman) #1 – no sugar, no grains, no legumes, no dairy products
2) Paleolithic (Caveman and Cavewoman) #2 – no sugar, no grains, no legumes, no dairy products, no beef or pork
3) Atkins Diet Program #1 – low carbohydrate, high fat, high protein
4) Atkins Diet Program #2 – low carbohydrate, high fat, high protein but no beef, pork or dairy products
5) Seafood, Fruit and Vegetables
6) Seafood and Vegetables (no fruit)
7) Vegetarian #1 – whole grains, legumes, vegetables, fruit
8) Vegetarian #2 – whole grains, legumes, vegetables, no fruit
9) Vegetarian #3 – no grains except for rice, legumes, vegetables, fruit
10) Vegetarian #4 – no grains except for rice, legumes, vegetables, no fruit
11) Raw Food Diet - with nuts and seeds for protein, no meat
12) Raw Food Diet – with cooked poultry and/or fish for protein
13) Calorie Counting – 2400 calories/day; 2100 calories/day; 1800 calories/day; 1500 calories/day; 1200 calories/day (test the daily caloric intake)
14) Low Fat – no fats, no extracted oils, low fat meats, low fat foods
15) Grapefruit and Egg Diet
16) Gluten and Dairy-Free Diet
17) Low Acid Diet – avoid acetic, citric, arachadonic, phosphoric and oxalic acids.
18) Food Combining – Do not combine meat with grains. Do not combine citrus fruits with grains.
19) Alternating Paleolithic Diet #1 with Vegetarian Diet #1 (in 2 to 4 day cycles)
20) Candida Program – no sugar, wheat, dried fruit, caffeine, beer or wine

List Of Cleanses

21) Master Cleanser – maple syrup, lemon juice, cayenne pepper and water. 3 day, 7 day or 10 day
22) Grape Juice Diet – white grape juice or purple grape juice
23) Vegetable Juice Fast – carrot, celery, beet, parsley, spinach, cabbage, tomatoes
24) Three Day Apple Fast
25) Liver Flush – olive oil, lemon juice and castor oil packs

Eat Organic

Diet Plan Details

1) Paleolithic #1

The Paleolithic diet is based on the fact that our ancestors had very few chronic diseases, ate indigenous foods and exercised daily (see Chapter One). This program restricts all sugars, any kind of grains, pasta or flours (gluten and non-gluten), legumes and all dairy products. You can eat all fruit, all vegetables including potatoes, lean meats, eggs and healthy fats such as olive oil, flax seed oil and grapeseed oil. You may also include fruit and vegetable juices. This diet program excels in promoting weight loss, healing digestive disorders, blood sugar disorders, diabetes, metabolic syndrome, chronic fatigue and a host of other health conditions.

2) Paleolithic #2

This program is the same as #1 except that beef and pork are eliminated as a protein choice. Certain health conditions are sensitive to beef (heart problems, high blood pressure, diabetes, cancer and arthritis for example) and the program works better without it.

3) Atkins Diet Program #1

This program often comes up for those people who have a very high intolerance to carbohydrates and suffer from fatigue, diabetes, heart disease, metabolic syndrome, depression, mood swings, water retention, weight gain and an inability to lose weight. The high fat in this diet helps to stabilize blood sugar levels and to ensure satiety to control hunger. It is a somewhat extreme program but works very well for the carbohydrate intolerant. If weight loss plateaus at some point, then it is necessary to calorie count. Follow the Atkins Plan as outlined in the book titled Dr. Atkins New Diet Revolution. Don't use this program permanently. Stay on it until the blood sugar hormones have stabilized and general health improves, which may take a few weeks. You may then transition to the Paleolithic diet programs. It is also recommended that many of you seek treatment for a carbohydrate addiction. (See Food Addictions - Chapter Two)

4) Atkins Diet Program #2

Use the same program as Atkins #1, but eliminate all dairy products, beef and pork. This helps to keep the diet less acidic and reduces over-all saturated fat intake.

5) Seafood, Fruit and Vegetables

This is a nice cleansing diet promoting weight loss, good nutrition and light energy. Eat all fruit, all vegetables and whatever seafood that you like and tolerate - fish and shellfish. Fruit and vegetables can be eaten raw or cooked. No other food groups are to be eaten on this program. Two to four weeks is an appropriate length of time for this program.

6) Seafood and Vegetables without Fruit

This is the same program as #5 except without fruit. Eliminating fruit intensifies and purifies the cleansing process and helps to stabilize erratic blood sugar levels. Two to four weeks is an appropriate length of time for this program as well.

7) Vegetarian #1

Eat whole grains, legumes, vegetables, fruit, nuts, seeds and soy products. This diet plan implies a strict vegetarian program without dairy products or eggs. It is also advisable to avoid wheat flour. Ensure that lots of vegetables are eaten; don't rely on just grains and legumes. Vegetarianism is very useful in balancing excessive meat eaters and high fat eaters and helps to prevent and heal those conditions most associated with heavy meat eating: heart disease, high blood pressure, arthritis, diabetes and cancer. However, it is recommended that in all but a few cases that this program not be permanent. (See Vegetarians – Chapter One)

8) Vegetarian #2
Eat whole grains, legumes, vegetables, fruit, nuts, seeds and soy products. This is the same program as #7, except all fruit is eliminated. This helps to stabilize blood sugar and reduce acidity. It is recommended that this program not be permanent – listen to your body.

9) Vegetarian #3
Eat legumes, vegetables, fruit, nuts, seeds, soy products and non-gluten grains such as rice, buckwheat, and bulgar. This program allows for the benefits of a vegetarian program without aggravating people who are sensitive to glutens and grain fibre. It is recommended that this program not be permanent – listen to your body.

10) Vegetarian #4
Eat legumes, vegetables, nuts, seeds, soy products and rice. No grains except for rice are allowed. Eliminate all fruit. This is a short-term program only for 2-3 weeks.

11) Raw Food Diet #1
This diet includes fruits, vegetables, juices, nuts, coconut milk, seeds, sprouted beans, sprouted grains, and healthy oils. This is an excellent cleansing program for improving digestion, increasing food enzymes and acquiring superior nutrition from your food. (Be cautious with eating lots of nuts – they can be highly allergenic). Similar to vegetarianism, the raw food diet is not recommended as a permanent program.

12) Raw Food Diet #2
This is the same plan as #1 but with cooked meat for protein, including eggs, fish and poultry, but no beef or pork. All the same foods can be eaten as Raw Food Diet #1 however flesh protein is added to maximize protein levels for the physically active, athletes, or other people who have a high requirement for protein. It is still an excellent cleansing program and is tolerated for longer periods of time than Raw Food Diet #1.

13) Calorie Counting
Most people will test for daily calories between 1200 and 2400. Calorie counting diets should be balanced daily by using all the food groups. Choose from light flesh proteins, eggs, whole grains, fruits and vegetables. Avoid all processed foods, sugar, white flours, junk food and anything else that isn't good for you – read Chapter 1.

14) Low-fat
Eliminate all added fats, extracted oils, high fat meat and dairy products. This diet should be considered an alarm bell for the damage that dietary fats are causing to the internal

organs, including the colon, heart, arteries, lymph system, liver and brain. Eat absolutely no fats or oils except for the ones that are naturally occurring in foods – no bottled oils, margarine, deep-fried foods, oil extracts or foods containing high levels of oils such as baked goods, pizzas and salad dressings. Also avoid beef, pork, bacon, poultry skin and high-fat dairy products. Eggs are okay if eaten with a soft yolk. Rely on whole grains, seeds, nuts, avocado, coconut and other fruit and vegetables for natural fat sources. Food intolerances and allergies often disappear on this program because fats create a barrier around other foods preventing proper digestion. Lowering dietary fats will improve the immune system. (See Fats and Oils under Common Food Problems – Repeat Offenders in Chapter 2).

15) Grapefruit and Egg Diet

This diet originated at the Mayo Clinic and relies on eggs to provide a daily complete protein and on grapefruit to stabilize blood sugar levels, regulate insulin levels and encourage weight loss by burning fat. It is one of the most effective weight loss programs and it decreases food cravings considerably.

- Breakfast and lunch consists of two eggs at each meal. Breakfast or lunch (but not both) can be accompanied by bacon or un-pasteurized cheese. Eat vegetables with any meal.

Supper consists of flesh protein (fish, poultry, beef, or pork) with unlimited quantities of vegetables. Be creative with cooking proteins – poached fish, tuna salads, chicken salads, roasted or grilled chicken and turkey, vege-table-meat stews, roasted meats, barbequed skewers etc.

- Drink one glass of grapefruit juice or eat ½ grapefruit with every meal (three times daily). Do not eat in between meals.

- Drink a glass of organic soy milk or tomato juice as a bedtime snack.

- Fats and oils such as butter, olive oil and grapeseed oil are allowed. No fruit or fruit juice should be eaten at any time. No grains, flours, pasta, potatoes, or sweet potatoes are allowed. Decaf coffee and/or herbal teas can be consumed for liquids. Drink plenty of good water.

- This program should be followed for 12 days on, then 2 days off, then repeat until you are at your desired weight.

- Eggs can be cooked any style – scrambled, boiled, fried, devilled, poached, egg salads or vegetable omelettes. If 4 eggs per day become difficult to do, exchange the lunch eggs with a low-fat flesh protein. This diet plan is not suitable for those people who are egg intolerant or for those who are sensitive to citric acid or grapefruit.

16) Dairy and Gluten Free

This diet plan is followed with the intent of removing major food intolerances, leading to the improvement of a number of allergy symptoms and health problems (see Chapter Two). All foods are allowed except for gluten-containing grains (rye, oats, wheat and barley) and dairy products – milk, cheese, yoghurt, sour cream and ice-cream. Small amounts of butter are often tolerated.

17) Low Acid Diet
Eliminating dietary acids (acetic, citric, arachadonic, phosphoric and oxalic acids) virtually eradicates or considerably reduces all body pain affecting joints, bones, muscles and connective tissue. It can also improve a variety of other health problems including kidney stones, skin problems, osteoarthritis, immune problems and a host of other nondescript or unexplained health symptoms.
- Eliminate citrus fruit, vinegar, sugar, potatoes, beef, and soft drinks.
- Eliminate foods high in oxalic acids, especially coffee, chocolate, nuts, rhubarb, spinach, strawberries, citrus peel, beets, olives, black tea and draft or canned beer.
- Drink alkaline water sold by water depots or from your own machine – don't use alkalizing drops sold as a water additive.

18) Food Combining
This is a good basic program for improving the digestion, and relieving stress on the stomach, pancreas, small intestine and liver. The following two food combinations can also be responsible for a variety of allergy symptoms but are often well hidden, as most people don't make the association:
a) Do not combine flesh meat with grains. Each meal should consist of either meat or grains but not both. For example, do not combine fish, poultry or beef with any grains including rice, wheat, bread, pasta, oats, barley, buckwheat, or quinoa in the same meal. Either eat meat or grains but not together - no meat sandwiches, bread with a meat meal,

chicken or fish with rice, chicken wraps, meatballs with pasta and so on. Eggs are not a flesh protein and potatoes are not a grain; therefore both of them can be combined with any foods. The meat-grain combination in the same meal, or even the same day, can cause digestive distress and a variety of other health symptoms.

b) Do not combine citrus fruits (grapefruit, oranges, pineapple, or lemon) with grains of any kind. No orange juice with oatmeal or cereal or a grapefruit with a sandwich, for example. Citrus fruit and grains in the same meal often cause stomach upsets and indigestion.

19) Alternating Paleolithic Diet #1 with Vegetarian Diet #1
Alternate the Paleolithic Diet #1 with the Vegetarian Diet #1 in 2 to 4 day cycles. In other words, test for how many days to stay on each diet before switching to the alternate. This is a useful program for those people who need more variety or need a balance between a high fibre program and a high protein program.

20) Candida Albicans Program (The Yeast Syndrome)
Candida Albicans is a naturally occurring yeast growth normally found in the human intestinal tract. In most cases, yeast lives in balance and in harmony with a variety of other intestinal organisms, including bacteria and viruses. However, due to modern diets and certain medications, yeast cells in the colon begin to reproduce abnormally creating an imbalance within the host's intestinal

ecosystem and consequently creating illness. Antibiotics, steroids, cortisone, oral contraceptives and hormone replacement therapy all encourage yeast overgrowth.

Once Candida gains a foothold in the intestinal tract it overtakes friendly bacteria, such as acidophilus or bifidus, produces acids and toxins and causes digestive complaints such as bloating, excessive gas, constipation, and/or diarrhea. Eventually the colon membranes become damaged ("leaky gut") and the Candida (now a fungus) migrates to other locations such as the vagina, bladder, sinuses, ears, lungs and skin. Acetaldehyde, a Candida toxin, has a marked effect on the body including hot flushes, increased heart rate with palpitations, low blood pressure, bronchial constriction, nausea and headaches. It also interferes with brain chemistry resulting in poor memory, feelings of being "spaced out" or drunk, depression and anxiety. It is interesting to note that acetaldehyde is a by-product of alcohol metabolism – it is therefore the main chemical that causes hangovers. All symptoms become possible with Candida stemming from liver toxicity, poor immunity, hormone imbalances, digestive problems, skin conditions, joint and muscle pain, and chronic fatigue.

Since Candida is caused by excessive dietary sugars and carbohydrates leading to colon toxicity, it is necessary to change the diet to discourage the growth of yeast. The appropriate supplements are required to "kill off" yeast cells. There may be a short "die-off" period in the beginning during which time people may experience temporary un-wellness as toxins and acids are released and eliminated. People normally start to feel better anywhere from 3 - 14 days after beginning the following program.

Eliminate all sugars, wheat products, dried fruit, fruit juice, beer, wine and caffeine. Keep flours to a minimum. Use pure maple syrup for an occasional sweetener. Avoid using honey or molasses. You may eat fresh fruit unless you have a blood sugar problem.

Contrary to popular opinion it is not necessary to eliminate foods that are associated with mold and fungus – Candida is not fed by either of these; Candida is fed by sugars and refined carbohydrates! The only time that mold-related foods ever need to be eliminated is in the case of a specific allergy or intolerance. You may therefore eat mushrooms, lemons, soy sauce, avocado, melons, etc.

Cleansing Plan Details

21) Master Cleanser
This cleanse consists of combining maple syrup, lemon juice, water and cayenne pepper and drinking 6-12 (8-10 oz) glasses per day for a total of 3, 7 or 10 days. It's a good cleanse for intestinal ulcers, colon cleansing, flushing kidney and liver toxins, decongestion, neutralizing acids and waste products, and initiating weight loss. Many conditions caused by toxins and acids will ameliorate during this cleanse.

Mix together and drink:

2 tbsp of organic lemon juice (freshly squeezed if possible)

2 tbsp of organic maple syrup (pure without

added sugar)

$\frac{1}{10}$ teaspoon cayenne pepper

1 cup clean water (preferably alkaline)

You may also drink extra water and herbal teas. It is recommended that you brush your teeth several times per day to prevent any erosion of tooth enamel by the citric acid in the lemon juice. See "Recommended Reading" for more details.

22) Grape Juice Diet

Grapes are wonderfully therapeutic and rich in tannins, polyphenols and antioxidants. They are anti-viral, anti-bacterial and anti-carcinogenic and thus have a reputation of benefit in many ailments including cancer. Test for white or purple grape juice and use organic grapes if you can find them. The grape program consists of a 12 hour fast each night from 8:00 pm to 8:00 am whereby only water is drank. From 8:00 a.m. to 8:00 p.m. only grape juice and/or grapes are consumed. The overnight water fast ensures that the cells are ready to uptake the therapeutic agents in the grapes. See "Recommended Reading" for reference material.

23) Vegetable Juice Fast

Freshly prepared juices are rich in live enzymes and nutrients. Juice fasts break down toxic materials, eliminate acids, stimulate new cell growth, increase the absorption of nutrients, and cleanses the elimination organs, including the skin. Choose from organic carrots, celery, beets, parsley, cabbage, cucumber, broccoli, tomatoes, wheatgrass and greens such as kale and spinach. You may also add garlic and/or ginger. Drink 6-8

(8 oz) glasses per day. You may eat raw vegetables as well.

24) Three Day Apple Fast

Apples, another therapeutic food, are amazing cleansers. Apple peels are very high in pectin, a soluble fibre. An apple fast will cleanse the colon, stimulate liver bile, eliminate heavy metals, neutralize excess acids and improve conditions of auto-intoxication (see "Leaky Gut" – Chapter 2). Eat nothing but organic apples all day and every day for 3 days. Drink plenty of good water (preferably alkaline) and each evening have the following drink: mix 1 cup of organic apple juice with 1 tablespoon of fresh lemon juice, 1 tablespoon of extra virgin olive and 1 clove of mashed raw garlic.

25) Liver Flush

The traditional liver flush was primarily used to eliminate gallstones, as a method of avoiding surgery. A liver flush is also a very useful way to cleanse and detoxify the liver by breaking up toxins, congestion, stones, and fatty deposits. Aside from the traditional liver flush method, I have also included a modified flush for those people who are more sensitive and prefer a more gentle, yet effective approach. Test for both.

Method A

- Day 1

Drink as much diluted apple juice as possible all day. Dilute apple juice with 50% clean, pure water. Eat very lightly – only fruit and vegetables, preferably raw.

Take the following supplements twice daily on all 3 days:

Bentonite Clay, Herbal Fibre or Psyllium Seed
Dandelion Root Tea
Black Radish (juice or ampules)

- Day 2
Until 5:00 p.m., drink diluted apple juice only
Don't ingest anything from 5:00 p.m. until 8:00 p.m., except water.
Then measure out:
1 - 1 ½ cups extra virgin olive oil
1- 1 ½ cups freshly squeezed lemon juice
Take 3 Tablespoons of each starting with the olive oil; repeat every 15 minutes until finished – about 3 hours. (If the olive oil becomes difficult to drink – try it with a straw).
**You may become nauseous during the night or the next morning although generally this will dissipate with the first bowel movement. Check the stool for gallstones and/or cholesterol balls.

Day 3
Eat very lightly – fruits, vegetables and light proteins

Method B
Start with a 4 day cleansing diet, eating only vegetables, vegetable juice, fish, and whole grains such as brown rice, bulgar, or buckwheat. Eliminate all sugar, fruit, flours, fats, meat, caffeine and alcohol. Drink plenty of water and/or herbal teas.

Take the following supplements twice daily on all 4 days of the cleansing diet:
Bentonite Clay, Herbal Fibre or Psyllium Seed
Dandelion Root Tea
Black Radish (juice or ampules)

Every night for 4 nights drink the following combination:
¼ cup of light olive oil,
2 tbsp of fresh lemon juice,
1-2 teaspoons of minced raw garlic
1/10 teaspoon of cayenne pepper.
Every night for 4 nights, apply a castor oil pack over the liver on the lower right hand side of the abdomen over the rib cage. See the Appendix for details.

And Now...
Chapter 8 provides us with an overview and reference guide for specific health problems and a comprehensive program to restore abundant health. Enjoy...

Love Your Body – It has a Soul

Chapter 8

REFERENCE GUIDE to HEALTH CONDITIONS
- Be Healthy -

As I have pointed out throughout this book, each person is very individual with unique constitutions, biochemistry, health conditions, nutritional and lifestyle requirements and dietary needs. Natural health practitioners treat people, not diseases. It is always best to customize an individual health program by using kinesiology to access the knowledge within the subconscious and beyond. However, over my more than twenty years of practice, there were certain patterns that emerged for most health conditions. I would like to share these highly successful health programs not only to build the reader's knowledge base, but also to provide help and support to those many people who don't have access to kinesiology or other health therapies and who would like to get started on programs that work.

I have formulated the programs in this chapter to be followed in their entirety – unless you are sensitive or intolerant to any of the recommended foods or remedies.

You will notice that the food culprits identified as being the most detrimental can often be the same from one health ailment to another. The nutritional information in Chapters 1 and 2 makes this rationale clear; it provides you with the fundamental knowledge as to why this is and also explains why eliminating problem foods are so critical to the success of any health program.

Results may be limited if the food programs are only followed in part. For a more specific diet plan, test for the appropriate program in Chapter 7. The dosages indicated are adult dosages – adjust accordingly for children. Dosages for herbs should be taken as directed on the package label.

Read on and enjoy the freedom of good health!

Agoraphobia

Foods to Eliminate:
Dairy products, wheat products, caffeine

Daily Nutrients:
Calcium citrate or coral calcium – 200 - 300 mg taken at bedtime
Magnesium citrate or aspartate – 300 - 500 mg taken in the morning

Herbs:
Passion Flower, Skullcap, Lemon Balm

Homeopathic Remedies:
Combination Tissue Salts 6x – Kali phos, Mag phos, Nat mur, Silicea – one dose three to four times daily or as needed.

Phosphorus 1M – one dose daily for 4 days
Aconitum 1M – one dose daily for 4 days

Lifestyle:
Meditation and Relaxation Exercises
Emotional Kinesiology

Allergies - Food

Foods to Eliminate:
All grains and grain products (wheat, spelt, kamut, oats, barley, rye, rice, buckwheat, quinoa, bulgar, etc.)
All known food allergens (see Chapter 2).

Daily Nutrients:
Probiotics - as directed on label
Beta-carotene - 25,000 IU daily
Liquid Iron - as directed on label
Selenium - 200 mcg
Drink alkaline water - 2-3 glasses

Herbs:
Psyllium Seed, Flax Seed (crushed)

Homeopathic Remedies:
Arnica 200c – one dose once or twice daily as needed for allergic reactions
Adrenaline 200c – one dose once or twice daily as needed for allergic reactions.
Thymus 200c – one dose daily for 14 days
Adrenal 200c – one dose daily for 14 days
Sulphur 200c – one dose daily for 7 days (fat intolerances)

Lifestyle:
Don't let your food victimize you
Check thyroid function

Allergies - Anaphylactic

Foods to Eliminate:
All known food allergens
Caffeine, dairy products, wheat, sugar, nuts

Daily Nutrients:
Liquid Iodine – 2 drops daily
Liquid Iron – take as directed on label

Homeopathic Remedies:
Use this protocol for building up the
immune system. Repeat as necessary.
Adrenalinum 1M - one dose daily for 4 days
Apis 1M - one dose daily for 4 days
Arnica 1M - one dose daily for 4 days
Thymuline 1M - one dose daily for 4 days

Lifestyle:
Check thyroid function.
Be aware of emotional "over-reactions"
Face up to challenges rather than avoid them

Allergies - Inhalant (dust, molds, pollens, animals)

Foods to Eliminate:
Dairy products, wheat products, sugar

Daily Nutrients:
Beta-carotene - 25,000 IU daily
Liquid Iron - as directed on label
Selenium - 200 mcg
Vitamin C – 2,000 mg daily

Homeopathic Remedies:
Dust 200c – one dose daily for 4 days (for
dust allergies)

Mold combination 200c – one dose daily for
4 days (for mold allergies)
Pollens 200c – one dose daily for 4 days (for
pollen allergies)
Sulphur 200c – one dose daily for 4 days
Thymuline, 1M – one dose daily for 14 days
If necessary repeat the specific remedies for
another 4 day cycle
For cat, dog and horse allergies use
homeopathic dilutions of the animal dander
in a 200c – one dose daily for 4 days – and
repeat as necessary

Lifestyle:
Deal with unexpressed anger and/or
suppressed grief
Believe that the world is a safe place

Anxiety and Obsessive Compulsive Disorder (OCD)

Foods to Eliminate:
All dairy products, all wheat products,
caffeine

Daily Nutrients:
Calcium citrate or Coral Calcium – 200 - 300
mg taken at bedtime
Magnesium citrate or aspartate – 300 - 500
mg taken in the morning
Herbs:
Passion Flower, Skullcap, Lemon Balm

Homeopathic Remedies:
Combination Tissue Salts 6x – Kali phos,
Mag phos, Nat mur, Silicea - one dose three
to four times daily or as needed
Aconitum 1M – one dose daily for 4 days

Arsenicum 200c – one dose daily for 5 days (repeat if necessary)
Phosphorus 1M – One dose daily for 4 days (repeat if necessary)
Phosphoric Acid 1M – One dose daily for 4 days (use for nervous burn-out, over-work)

Flower Essences:
Five-Flower Formula, Aspen, Chamomile, Cherry plum, Vervain

Lifestyle:
Meditation and Relaxation Exercises
Emotional Kinesiology
Get enough sleep

Arthritis - Osteoarthritis and Osteoporosis

Foods to Eliminate:
Dairy products, beef, potatoes, sugar, fruit, nuts, caffeine, soft drinks

Daily Nutrients:
Calcium citrate or aspartate – 2 capsules at bedtime
Vitamin B6 – 200 mg
MSM – 2,000 mg
Coenzyme Q10 – 100 mg
Fish oils – as directed on label
Horsetail – 500 mg daily for 30 days
Alkaline water - 2-3 glasses

Herbs:
Comfrey Root Tincture

Homeopathic Remedies:
Take each remedy separately, in succession

- in the order below - with 7 days between each remedy.
Calc Carb 200c – one dose daily for 4 days
Calc Fluor 200c – one dose daily for 4 days
Calc Phos 200c – one dose daily for 4 days
Ruta Grav 200c – one dose daily for 4 days
Silicea 200c – one dose daily for 4 days

Lifestyle:
Weight-bearing exercises such as weight-training and yoga are the most beneficial exercises for retaining and re-building bone density
Regular exercise such as walking, swimming, biking and stretching
Use a Vibration Exercise Machine
Lose weight – excess weight strains joints and causes inflammation
Maintain purpose in your life
Be emotionally flexible; don't get set in your ways

Arthritis - Rheumatoid Arthritis

Foods to Eliminate:
Dairy products, wheat products, sugar, fruit, potatoes, tomatoes, soft drinks

Daily Nutrients:
Probiotics - take as directed on label
Calcium citrate or aspartate - 2 capsules at bedtime
Selenium - 200 mcg
Folic acid - 3 mg
Fish oils - take as directed on label
Liquid Iodine - 2 drops daily

Herbs:
Psyllium Seed, Slippery Elm, Yucca

Lifestyle:
Regular exercise, especially stretching
Express yourself, rather than punishing
yourself
Avoid internalizing what is bothering you
and stand up for yourself
Interact with your world - be the cause
rather than the effect

Asthma, Bronchitis, COPD and Chest Congestion

Foods to Eliminate:
Dairy products, wheat products, sugar,
citrus fruit, eggs

Daily Nutrients:
Beta-carotene 25,000 IU - twice daily
Liquid Iodine - 2 drops
Liquid Iron - as directed on label

Herbs:
Astragalus, Fenugreek, Licorice Root,
Lobelia, Reishi
Use mustard packs to break up chest
congestion

Homeopathic Remedies:
Adrenal, 200c – one dose daily for 14 days
Sulphur, 200c – one dose daily for 2 four-day
cycles (with 4 days in between each cycle)
Pulsatilla, 200c – one dose daily for 7 days
Silicea, 200c – one dose daily for 7 days
Nat sulph, 200c – one dose daily for 7 days
(Start with Adrenal and Sulphur; if further
remedies are required take Pulsatilla and
Silicea, then Nat Sulph)

Flower Essences:
Yerba Santa

Lifestyle:
Breathing Exercises
Heal grief and sadness

Attention Deficit (ADD), Attention Deficit with Hyperactivity (ADHD), Hyperactivity, Autism

Foods to Eliminate:
Dairy products, all glutens, caffeine, sugar,
eggs, food preservatives, additives and food
colourings

Daily Nutrients:
Mixed oils taken as directed (Efalex)
Evening primrose oil – 500 IU
Vitamin B12 – 500 mcg daily (sublingual)
Folic acid - 3 mg daily
Magnesium citrate or aspartate – 200 mg
daily
Calcium citrate – 200 mg daily
Liquid Iron as directed on label

Herbs:
Lemon, Passion Flower, Skullcap

Homeopathic Remedies:
Combination Tissue Salts 6x – Kali phos,
Mag phos, Nat mur, Silicea – one dose taken
three to four times daily or as needed
ADD – Silicea 1M – one dose daily for 3
days
Picric acid 1M – one dose daily for 3 days
ADHD – Tarantula 200c – one dose daily for
3 days

Chamomila 1M – one dose daily for 3 days
Phosphorus 1M – one dose daily for 7 days
Autism – Phosphorus 1M – one dose daily
for 7 days
Carcinosum 1M – one dose daily for 7 days
Natrum mur 1M – one dose daily for 2 days

Lifestyle:
Calm, supportive and positive environments
Meditation and Relaxation Exercises
For children ensure parental leadership
within the home
Play music

Back Pain

Foods to Eliminate:
Beef, potatoes, milk, sugar

Daily Nutrients:
Calcium citrate or Coral Calcium – 2
capsules at bedtime
Magnesium citrate or aspartate – 500 mg
Vitamin B5 – 500 mg

Herbs:
Comfrey Root Tincture, Valerian Root

Homeopathic Remedies:
Bryonia 1M – one dose daily for 4 days
Calc Carb, 200c – one dose daily for 4 days
Rhus-Tox 1M – one dose daily for 7 days

Lifestyle:
Back strengthening exercises
Use a Vibration Exercise Machine
Swimming and stretching
Lose belly fat - it pulls your back out of

alignment
Release work stress and irritation
Deal with feelings of betrayal

Bladder Infections (Cystitis)

Foods to Eliminate:
Caffeine, sugar, beer, dried fruit, soft drinks

Daily Nutrients:
Probiotics - as directed on label
Liquid Iodine – 4 drops daily
Liquid Iron - as directed on label

Herbs:
Goldenseal

Lifestyle:
Heal jealousies and insecurities
Absolutely no caffeine

Brain Disorders - Alzheimer's, Parkinson's, Dementia, Memory Loss and Poor Concentration

Foods to Eliminate:
Caffeine, sugar, wheat, bread, dairy products
Emphasize high protein, low-carbohydrate diets

Daily Nutrients:
Probiotics – take as directed on label
Vitamin B12 – 2,000 mcg (sublingual)
Vitamin E – 800 IU
Folic Acid – 6 mg
Phosphatidyl Choline – 2,000 - 2,400 mg
Phosphatidyl Serine – 200 mg
Selenium – 200 mg

Zinc citrate – 50 mg
Fish Oils – 2,000 mg

Herbs:
Fo-Ti, Gotu Kola

Homeopathic Remedies:
Combination Tissue Salts 6x – Calc Phos, Ferr Phos, Kali Phos, Mag Phos, Nat Phos - one dose – three times daily
Take in succession with 7 days in between each remedy
Alumina 1M – one dose daily for 7 days
Phosphorus 1M – one dose daily for 7 days
Hyoscamus 1M – one dose daily for 7 days
Picric Acid 1M – one dose daily for 7 days

Flower essences:
Clematis, Honeysuckle, Rabbitbrush, Rosemary

Lifestyle:
Cardiovascular exercise, preferably outdoors
Make an effort to remember and verbalize all of the unpleasant events from the past; then let them go
Heal resentment and bitterness
Learn a new language

Cancer - All Cancers
WEIGHT LOSS is an absolute must (see Chapter 1). Excess weight (even by 10-15 pounds) will continue to intoxicate the body, depress the immune system, stress the liver, and cause hormone imbalances.

DETOXIFICATION is an absolute must – it is the most successful approach in virtually all cancers.

Drink absolutely NO alcohol, caffeine or soft drinks; do NOT smoke (cigarettes or pot), and do NOT use drugs (unless they are prescription drugs that are required for serious health problems as determined by you and your doctor). All of these are major risk factors that you will not be able to over-come with good food or supplements.

Eat a raw food diet with vegetable juices and only small amounts of fish and seafood for protein, until remission. This is the best approach for all cancers in the active stage. However, for those people who find a raw food diet too difficult, are unable to thrive on raw food, or for those people who are in remission, I have made specific dietary suggestions for specific cancers below – also see Chapter 7 for information on specific diet programs.

All people preventing or working with cancer - on the raw food diet or not - should have the following:

Organic fruits and vegetables – as much as you can eat (eat like a rabbit)
Vegetable juices, freshly made 2-3 times daily
Vegetable broth 2-3 times per week
Drink alkaline water - 2-3 glasses daily
Colonic irrigations – between 6 and 12 sessions over 3 to 8 weeks
Regular exercise outdoors – cancer hates fresh air!
Visualizations to improve immunity and well-being
Positive attitude – about everything!
Stress management

Breast, Ovarian and Cervical

Foods to Eliminate:
Bottled oils or oil extracts, processed oils, mayonnaise or butter (Eat absolutely no fats or oils other than those naturally occurring in fruit, vegetables and light proteins)
Caffeine, beef, pork, poultry skin, dairy products
Sugar or grain flours of any kind
Increase fibre intake

Daily Nutrients:
Probiotics – take as directed on label
Selenium – 200 - 300 mcg
Liquid Iron as directed on label
Liquid Iodine – 4 drops
Zinc citrate - 25 mg
Vitamin E – 800 IU
Vitamin B6 - 100-200 mg
Folic acid - 4 mg
Methionine – 500 mg

Herbs:
Maitake, Shiitake, Dandelion Root, Echinacea, Goldenseal, Milk Thistle, Oregon grape Root, Psyllium Seed, Flax Seeds (crushed)

Homeopathic Remedies:
Thymuline 200c – one dose daily for 14 days - repeat every 2 months
Sulphur 1M – one dose daily for 10 - 14 days
Conium, 1M – one dose daily for 6 days (breast)
Phytolacca 1M – one dose daily for 14 days (breast only)
Silicea 1M – one dose daily for 2 four-day cycles (with 4 days in between each cycle)
Apis 1M – one dose daily for 4 days (ovarian only)

Lifestyle:
Heal a poor self-image
Heal themes of abuse, including sexual
Heal your anger and your judgments

Colon, Colorectal and Stomach Cancer

Foods to Eliminate:
Bottled oils or oil extracts, processed oils, mayonnaise or butter (Eat absolutely no fats or oils other than those naturally occurring in fruit, vegetables and light proteins)
Caffeine, beef, pork, poultry skin, dairy products
Sugar, grain flours of any kind
Emphasize low-fat, high-fibre

Daily Nutrients:
Probiotics – take as directed on label
Vitamin A – 10,000 IU
Vitamin B12 – 1,000 - 2,000 mcg
Folic Acid – 6 mg
Selenium – 200 - 300 mg
Liquid Iodine – 4 drops
Potassium – 100 mg

Herbs:
Psyllium Seed, Ginger, Aloe Vera, Slippery Elm, Chlorophyll, Flax Seeds (crushed), Raw Garlic

Homeopathic Remedies:
Nux-Vomica 1M – one dose daily for 7 days
Sulphur 1M – one dose daily for 7 days

Lifestyle:
Castor oil packs applied over the lower

abdomen for 4 consecutive nights every week for 2-3 weeks (See Appendix)
Deal with unhappy relationships and/or money worries (colon)
Heal addictions used to hide low self-esteem
Stop competing (stomach)

Liver Cancer

Foods to Eliminate:
Animal fat
Fats or bottled oils or oil extracts, processed oils, mayonnaise or butter (Eat absolutely no fats or oils other than those naturally occurring in fruit, vegetables and light proteins)
Caffeine, beef, pork, poultry skin and dairy products
Sugar and grain flours of any kind
Emphasize low-fat, high fibre

Daily Nutrients:
Vitamin B12 – 1,000 - 2,000 mcg
Vitamin B6 – 200 - 300 mg
Vitamin C – 4,000 mg
Folic Acid – 6 mg
Selenium – 200 - 300 mg
Liquid Iron – as directed on label
Methionine – 500 mg
Choline – 500 mg

Herbs:
Kelp, Golden seal, Dandelion Root, Milk Thistle, Ginger, Black Radish, Shiitake, Maitake, Astragalus, Flax Seed (crushed)

Homeopathic Remedies:
Take in succession with 7 days in between each one:

Nux-Vomica 1M – one dose daily for 7 days
Lycopodium 1M – one dose daily for 7 days
Sulphur 1M – one dose daily for 7 days
Staphysagria 1M – one dose daily for 5 days

Lifestyle:
Castor oil packs applied over the liver area for 4 consecutive nights every week for 3 weeks (See Appendix)
Heal your anger and love your liver
Manage stress levels

Lymphoma, Leukemia and Bone

Foods to Eliminate:
Bottled oils or oil extracts, processed oils, mayonnaise or butter (Eat absolutely no fats or oils other than those naturally occurring in fruit, vegetables and light proteins)
Beef, pork, poultry skin, dairy products
Caffeine and sugar

Daily Nutrients:
Beta-carotene - 50,000 IU
Vitamin C – 4,000 mg
Liquid Iodine – 4 drops
Selenium – 200 mcg
Zinc citrate – 50 mg

Herbs:
Reishi, Pau d'arco (tabeebo), Goldenseal, Echinacea, Oregon grape root, Yellow dock, Spirulina

Homeopathic Remedies:
Take each of these remedies for three 4-day cycles (with 4 days in between each cycle)
Thymus 200c

Spleen 200c

Lymph 200c

Take each of these remedies in succession in this order – with 7 days in between each one

Conium 1M – One dose daily for 4 days (lymphoma and bone)

Phytolacca 1M – One dose daily for 4 days (lymphoma and bone)

Silicea 1M – One dose daily for 7 days

Sulphur 1M – One dose daily for 7 days

Calc Fluor, 1M – One dose daily for 4 days (bone cancer only)

Symphytum, 1M – One dose daily for 7 days (bone cancer only)

Lifestyle:
Detoxification exercises – walking, lake or ocean swimming, outdoor biking, rebounding, and stretching

Vibration Exercise Machine

Lung Cancer

Foods to Eliminate:
Fats or bottled oils or oil extracts, processed oils, mayonnaise or butter (Eat absolutely no fats or oils other than those naturally occurring in fruit, vegetables and light proteins)

Beef, pork, poultry skin and dairy products

Caffeine and sugar

Daily Nutrients:
Beta-carotene - 50,000 IU

Vitamin C – 4,000 mg

Liquid Iodine – 4 drops

Liquid Iron – as directed on label

Selenium - 200 mg

Herbs:
Astragalus, Reishi, Lobelia, Mullein, Horehound, Coltsfoot

Homeopathic Remedies:
Silicea 1M – one dose daily for 7 days

Arsenicum 1M – one dose daily for 7 days

Lifestyle:
Breathing exercises

Clean Air

Heal residual sadness and grief

Pancreatic Cancer and Pancreatitis

Foods to Eliminate:
All grains, flours and sugar

Animal fat

Caffeine

Increase vegetable consumption

Emphasize low-carbohydrate diet

Daily Nutrients:
Probiotics – take as directed on label

Digestive enzymes with each meal as directed on label

Kelp – 1,000 mg

Vitamin B6 – 200 mg

Alpha-lipoic acid – 100 mg

Herbs:
Psyllium Seed, Flax Seeds (crushed), Ginger, Shiitake, Spirulina, Juniper Berry

Homeopathic Remedies:
Conium 1M – one dose daily for 4 days

Arsenicum 200c – one dose daily for 7 days

Phosphorus 1M – one dose daily for 7 days

Lifestyle:
Deal with resentment
Work on being patient
Don't be afraid of change or procrastinate on making life-altering changes

----

Prostate and Testicular Cancer (and Prostatitis)

Foods to Eliminate:
Caffeine, beef, dairy products (absolutely no caffeine, beef or dairy products)
Bottled oils or oil extracts, processed oils, mayonnaise or butter
Increase consumption of whole grains and vegetables
Emphasize low-fat, high-fibre

Daily Nutrients:
Probiotics – take as directed on label
Evening Primrose Oil – 2,000 IU
Vitamin E – 800 IU
Liquid Iodine – 4 drops
Selenium – 200 mcg
Zinc citrate – 50 mg
Lycopene – 10 - 15 mg

Herbs:
Saw Palmetto, Pygeum, Pumpkin Seeds, Psyllium Seed, Flax Seeds (crushed)
Homeopathic Remedies for prostate and testicular cancer:
Testes 200c – one dose daily for 14 days
Conium 1M– one dose daily for 14 days
Sulphur 1M – one dose daily for 14 days
Thuja 1M – one dose daily for 14 days

Lifestyle:
Exercise regularly
Deal with anger issues
Heal any sexual frustrations and/or feelings of inadequacy
Calm fantasies of excessive sexual aggression, if present

Skin Cancer

Foods to Eliminate:
Fats or bottled oils or oil extracts, processed oils, mayonnaise or butter (Eat absolutely no fats or oils other than those naturally occurring in fruit, vegetables and light proteins)
Beef, pork, poultry skin and dairy products
Sugar and caffeine
Increase vegetable consumption

Daily Nutrients:
Probiotics – take as directed on label
Beta-carotene – 50,000 IU
Folic Acid – 6 mg
Selenium – 200 mcg
Liquid Iodine – 2 drops
Zinc citrate – 50 mg

Herbs:
Green Tea, Red Clover, Chickweed, Plantain, Yellow dock, Psyllium Seed, Flax Seed (crushed)

Homeopathic Remedies:
Silicea 1M – one dose daily for 7 days
Sulphur 1M – one dose daily for 7 days
Thuja 1M – one dose daily for 7 days

Lifestyle:
No sunscreen of any kind
Wear light clothing and/or apply pure coconut oil
Believe that the world is a safe place
Believe that you are a good person and not a "monster"
Don't be afraid of the light – embrace it

Candida Albicans (The Yeast Syndrome)

Foods to Eliminate:
Sugar, wheat, dairy products, dried fruit, fruit juices, wine, beer
(See Chapter 7 for more information)

Daily Nutrients:
Probiotics – take as directed on label
Liquid Iodine – 4 drops daily

Herbs:
Psyllium Seed, Raw Garlic, Grapefruit Seed Extract, Pau D'arco

Homeopathic Remedies:
Candida 200C – one dose daily for 10-14 days

Lifestyle:
Exercise in the fresh air
Don't let yeast control your food cravings

Chronic Fatigue and/or Adrenal Burn-Out

Foods to Eliminate:
Caffeine, sugar, fruit, glutens, dairy products

Daily Nutrients:
Probiotics – take as directed on label
Liquid Iron – take as directed on label
Vitamin B5 – 500 mg
Vitamin B12 – 1,000 mcg (sublingual)
Folic Acid – 6 mg
Evening Primrose Oil – 2,000 IU
Spirulina – 3,000 mg – twice daily

Herbs:
Ashwaghanda, Ginseng, Licorice root,

Homeopathic Remedies:
Adrenal 200c – one dose daily for 14 days
Nux-vomica 200c – one dose daily for 10-14 days
Phosphoric Acid 1M - one dose daily for 7 days
If needed after the previous three:
Nat Mur 1M – one dose daily for 4 days
Silicea 1M – one dose daily for 7 days

Flower Essences:
Aloe Vera, Hornbeam, Olive

Lifestyle:
Heal past emotional traumas
Practice "non-attachment" – relationships, jobs and homes
Embrace change

Colds and Flus

Foods to Eliminate:
Dairy products, sugar

Daily Nutrients:
Vitamin A – 10,000 IU twice daily
Zinc citrate – 50 mg twice daily
Vitamin C – 2,000 mg – twice daily

Colloidal Silver – one dose as directed on label – twice daily
Olive oil – 1 tablespoon

Herbs:
Echinacea, Goldenseal, Astragalus, Ginger, Garlic

Homeopathic Remedies:
Influenzium 30c – one dose – twice daily
Thymuline, 30c – one dose – twice daily
Sulphur 30c – one dose – twice daily

Flower Essences:
Lavender

Lifestyle:
Pace yourself; slow down the frenetic "to do" list

Colitis, Irritable Bowel Syndrome (IBS), Diverticulitis and Constipation

Foods to Eliminate:
All grains (gluten and non-gluten), all dairy products
(Once symptoms have abated you may re-introduce non-gluten grains if tolerated)
Increase vegetable consumption, raw or cooked

Daily Nutrients:
Probiotics – take as directed on label
Vitamin B12 – 1,000 mcg
Folic acid – 3 mg
Coral calcium – 2 - 3 capsules daily
Olive Oil – 1 tablespoon daily
Alkaline water - 2-3 glasses

Herbs:
Aloe Vera Juice, Kelp, Slippery elm, Psyllium seed, Comfrey leaf, Ginger tea, Fennel tea, Peppermint tea, Flax Seed (crushed)

Homeopathic Remedies:
Arsenicum 200c – one dose daily for 7 days
Nux-Vomica 200c – one dose daily for 7 days
Sulphur 200c – one dose daily for 7 days

Flower Essences:
Chamomile, Dandelion

Lifestyle:
Castor oil packs applied over the lower abdomen for 4 consecutive nights every week for 2 weeks (See Appendix)
Heal personal relationships, both current and past
Deal with financial stress

Dental – Cavities, Abscesses, Malformation, Teething, Periodontal Disease

Foods to Eliminate:
Sugar, soft drinks, citrus fruit, vinegar, milk and refined carbohydrates (flours)

Daily Nutrients:
Calcium citrate or coral calcium – 2 capsules
Vitamin A – 10,000 IU daily
Fish Oil – as directed on label
Coenzyme Q10 – 100 mg (gum diseases)
Alkaline water – 2-3 glasses

Herbs:
Raw Garlic applied directly to the tooth (abscesses)

Homeopathic Remedies:
Calc Phos 200c – one dose daily for 7 days
Sulphur 1M – one dose daily for 7 days
Silicea 1M – one dose daily for 4 days
(abscesses)

Teething:
Combination Tissue Salts 6x – Calc Phos,
Calc Fluor, Ferr Phos, Mag Phos, Silicea

Lifestyle:
Brush and floss regularly
Emphasize eating vegetables
Heal old soul issues

Depression, including Situational, Clinical, Post-Partum and Seasonal Affective Disorder (SAD)

Foods to Eliminate:
Caffeine, sugar, wheat

Daily Nutrients:
Phenylalanine – 500 mg once or twice daily
Phosphatidyl Choline – 1,000 – 2,000 mg at
bedtime
Vitamin B12 – 1,000 mcg (sublingual)
Folic Acid – 3 mg
Liquid Iron – take as directed

Herbs:
St John's Wort, Ginseng

Homeopathic Remedies:
Ignatia 1M – one dose daily for 7 days (grief,
lost love)
Take each remedy separately, in succession
- in the order below - with 7 days between
each remedy
Nux-vomica 1M – one dose daily for 7 days
Nat Mur 1M – one dose daily for 4 days
Thuja 1M – one dose daily for 14 days

Flower Essences:
Borage, Gorse, Mustard, Sweet Chestnut,
Bleeding Heart

Lifestyle:
Daily exercise, preferably outside
Get at least 7-8 hours of sleep
Heal your anger: many depressions are
internalized anger
Don't wait for the situation to change;
change the situation
Do volunteer work with those who are less
fortunate

Diabetes Type 1 (Juvenile Diabetes)

Foods to Eliminate:
Sugar, fruit, fruit juice, caffeine, all dairy
products, all glutens

Daily Nutrients:
Probiotics – take as directed on label
Vitamin B6 – 25 – 50 mg daily
Coral Calcium – ½ capsule daily

Herbs:
Crushed flax seed

Homeopathic Remedies:
Insulin 30c – one dose daily for 14 days, or
as required
Alfalfa 30c – one dose twice daily for 7 days
Pancreas 200c – one dose daily for 14 days

Lifestyle:
Test for food allergies
Increase fibre – eat lots of vegetables!
Control stress levels

Diabetes Type 2 (Late Onset) and Insulin Resistance

Foods to Eliminate:
Caffeine, sugar, glutens, fruit, milk, alcohol
Emphasize low fat and high fibre
Don't skip meals nor allow yourself to get overly hungry

Daily Nutrients:
Probiotics – take as directed on label
Vitamin B6 – 250 mg
Chromium – 250 mcg (30 days only)
Alpha-Lipoic acid – 100 mg
Zinc citrate – 50 mg
Spirulina – 3,000 mg – twice daily

Herbs:
Juniper berry, Dandelion Root, Psyllium Seed, Flax Seed (crushed)

Homeopathic Remedies:
Alfalfa 30c – one dose twice daily for 7 days
Lycopodium 1M – one dose daily for 7 days
Sulphur 1M – one dose daily for 7 days
Pancreas 200c – one dose daily for 14 days
Insulin 30c – one dose daily for 14 days, or as required

Lifestyle:
Lose weight
Increase fibre
Control stress levels

Avoid over-working
Avoid deadlines and constant hurrying

Diarrhea

Foods to Eliminate:
Caffeine, sugar, fruit, fruit juice, dairy products, wheat
(Bananas and/or rice water can be beneficial)

Daily Nutrients:
Probiotics – take as direct on label
Vitamin B12 – 1,000 mcg (sublingual)
Folic Acid – 3 mg

Herbs:
Psyllium Seed, Aloe Vera Juice, Slippery Elm, Ginger Tea, Fennel Tea

Homeopathic Remedies:
Take this combination of remedies daily until the symptoms disappear (for no longer than 7 days)
Arsenicum 30c – twice daily for 7 days
Chamomila 30c – one dose twice daily
China 30c – one dose twice daily
Nux-vomica 30c – one dose twice daily
Sulphur 200c – one dose twice daily
Veratrum 30c – one dose twice daily

Flower Essences:
Chamomile, Five-Flower Formula, Larch

Lifestyle:
Fear of change; learn to embrace change – it's how we grow
Fear of judgment and inadequacy; realize

that we are all connected and that we are here to support one another

----

Eating Disorders, Bulimia and Anorexia

Foods to Eliminate:
Sugar, wheat, caffeine

Daily Nutrients:
Folic Acid – 3 mg
Vitamin B12 – 1,000 mcg (sublingual)
Vitamin E – 400 IU
Potassium – 100 mg
Spirulina – 2,000 mg – twice daily

Herbs:
Kelp, Catnip, Caraway
Homeopathic Remedies:
Ignatia 1M – one dose daily for 7 days
Nat Mur 1M – one dose daily for 4 days
Staphysagria 1M – one dose daily for 4 days

Flower Essences:
Cherry plum, Crab apple, Evening primrose, Holly, Pretty face, Willow

Lifestyle:
It is no longer necessary to defy and take revenge on a controlling family member or partner by threatening to die. You are your own person with the power to love yourself. Choose self-love over anger, self-punishment and punishing others.
Heal suppressed anger!

Epilepsy

Foods to Eliminate:
Caffeine, sugar, glutens
Emphasize high protein, low carbohydrates

Daily Nutrients:
Copper – 5 mg
Evening Primrose Oil – 1,000 IU
Magnesium – 300 mg - twice daily
Manganese – 10 mg
Zinc citrate – 10 mg
Vitamin B6 – 250 - 500 mg
Vitamin B12 – 2,000 mcg
Vitamin E – 800 IU
Phosphatidyl Choline – 1,000 mg at bedtime

Herbs:
Passion flower, Skullcap, Valerian root

Homeopathic Remedies:
Combination Tissue Salts 6x – Calc Phos, Ferr Phos, Kali Phos, Mag Phos, Nat Phos one dose as directed 4 times daily
Belladonna 1M – one dose daily for 4 days (repeat as necessary)
Cuprum Met 200c – one dose daily for 4 days
Mag Phos 1M – one dose daily for 7-10 days (repeat as necessary)
Sulphur, 1M – one dose daily for 7 days

Flower Essences:
Five-Flower Formula, Ladyslipper, Star of Bethlehem

Lifestyle:
Be cautious of low blood sugar problems – see "Hypoglycemia"

Let go of control or get out of controlling situations
Recognize hidden fears

Fibrocysts

Foods to Eliminate:
Caffeine, black tea, beef and dairy products
Increase fibre

Daily Nutrients:
Vitamin E – 400 IU
Liquid Iodine – 2 drops daily

Herbs:
Flax Seeds (crushed) – 1-2 tablespoons

Homeopathic Remedies:
Calc Phos 200c – one dose daily for 4 days
Phytolacca 200c – one dose daily for 4 days
Silicea 200c - one dose daily for 4 days

Lifestyle:
Be comfortable with your sexuality

Food Poisoning - Acute and Chronic

Foods to Eliminate:
Sugar, all meat
Emphasize cooked vegetables and vegetable soups

Daily Nutrients:
Probiotics – as directed on label
Vitamin B12 - 2,000 mcg (sublingual)
Folic Acid – 3 mg
Spirulina – 3,000 mg

Herbs:
Ginger, Garlic
For acute symptoms take 1-2 oz of straight liquor such as vodka, gin, rye, scotch, or rum

Homeopathic Remedies:
Arsenicum 200c – one dose twice daily as needed
Nux-vomica 1M – one dose daily for 3 days
Homeopathic nosode specific to the type of bacteria, such as Salmonella, E Coli, or Botulinum, 200c Take the correct remedy one dose twice daily until symptoms abate

Lifestyle:
Deal with emotional shock
Deal with change

Headaches

Foods to Eliminate:
Caffeine, sugar, dairy products, glutens, nuts

Daily Nutrients:
Probiotics – take as directed on label
Vitamin B12 – 1,000 mcg (sublingual)
Magnesium citrate or aspartate – 300-500 mg

Herbs:
Chamomile, Lemon balm, Passion flower, Skullcap, Valerian Root

Homeopathic Remedies:
Gelsemium 1M – one dose daily for 4 days (head injuries or headaches with vertigo)
Lachesis 1M – one dose daily for 7 days (PMS or menopausal headaches)
Nat Mur 1M – one dose daily for 4 days

(chronic and emotional)
Nux-Vomica 1M – one dose daily for 7 days
(toxic headaches)
Sulphur 1M – one dose daily for 7 days
(toxic headaches)

Flower Essences:
Centaury, Chamomile, Five-Flower Formula, Pink Yarrow

Lifestyle:
Stress-relieving exercises, stretching, meditation
Learn to live your own life, to say no and to make your own decisions
Don't be a martyr
Watch for the tendency to take on other people's problems

Heartburn, Indigestion, Hiatus Hernias and Ulcers

Foods to Eliminate:
Caffeine, soft drinks, sugar, wheat or bread
Emphasize light proteins and vegetables

Daily Nutrients:
Probiotics – as directed on label
Folic Acid – 6 mg
Potassium – 100 mg
Magnesium – 300 mg
Liquid Iodine – 2 drops
Herbs:
Slippery elm, Marshmallow Root, Mastica chios, Ginger, Comfrey Leaf

Homeopathic Remedies:
Nux-Vomica 200c – one dose daily for 10 days

Pulsatilla 200c – one dose daily for 7 days
Calc Carb 200c – one dose daily for 4 days
Nat Phos 200c – one dose daily for 4 days

Flower Essences:
Lavender, Impatiens, Elm

Lifestyle:
Deal with anticipation anxiety, deadlines, and feelings of being trapped. Feeling trapped is a mindset – there is always a way out when you get out of your own way. Control worrying - worrying is like praying for the things that you don't want to have happen.

Heart and Cardiovascular Disease

Food to Eliminate:
Caffeine, alcohol, sugar, dairy products, beef, pork, poultry
Eat only fish, and eggs with a soft yolk (2-3 per week)
Emphasize high fibre grains and vegetables

Daily Nutrients:
Vitamin B6 – 250 mg
Vitamin B12 – 1,000 mcg (sublingual)
Folic Acid – 6 mg
Fish Oil – 1,000 mg
Coenzyme Q10 – 100 mg
Magnesium citrate – 300 mg
Potassium – 200 mg
Vitamin E – 400 IU (use caution with high blood pressure)
Choline – 500 mg
Carnitine – 500 mg

Herbs:
Garlic, Cayenne Pepper, Hawthorne Berry, Flax Seed (crushed)

Homeopathic Remedies:
Lachesis 200c – one dose daily for 7 days
Naja 200c – one dose daily for 4 days

Flower Essences:
Holly, Calendula, Mallow

Lifestyle:
Lose weight
Regular cardiovascular exercise
Alleviate stress
Get your priorities straight and open your heart. Warm up and melt the ice. The most important thing in our lives is for each and every one of us to bond and connect with one another – at the heart level. Be warm, fuzzy and compassionate. Replace anger with love.

Hypoglycemia (Low Blood Sugar)

Foods to Eliminate:
Caffeine, sugar, wheat, all flours, beer and wine
Eat regular meals containing at least one serving of protein

Daily Nutrients:
Probiotics – take as directed on label
Vitamin B6 – 250 mg
Magnesium citrate or aspartate – 300-500 mg
Spirulina – 3,000 mg twice daily

Herbs:
Flax Seed (crushed), Psyllium Seed, Licorice

Root (blood sugar)
Chamomile, Skullcap, Passion Flower, Lemon Balm (nervous tension)

Homeopathic Remedies:
Pancreas 200c – one dose daily for 7 days
Sulphur 200c – one dose daily for 7 days

Flower Essences:
Aspen, Five-Flower Formula

Lifestyle:
Relaxation exercises for nervous tension
Heal depression; experience more joy
Be happy

Kidney Stones

Foods to Eliminate:
Sugar, soft drinks, wheat, dairy products, beef
Reduce oxalic acid found especially in rhubarb, spinach, strawberries, citrus peel, coffee, chocolate, nuts, beets, black tea and draft or canned beer (See Chapter 2 – "oxalic acids")

Daily Nutrients:
Magnesium citrate or aspartate – 500 mg
Potassium - 200 mg
Vitamin B6 - 100 mg
Probiotics - as directed
Lemon juice - 1 tablespoon daily (acute), 1 teaspoon daily (prevention)
Drink alkaline water - 2-3 glasses

Herbs:
Juniper berry, Uva Ursi, Dandelion Leaf,

Marshmallow Root

Homeopathic Remedies:
Colocynthis 1M – one dose daily for 4 days
Silicea 1M – one dose daily for 4 days
Sulphur 1M – one dose daily for 4 days
Berberis 30C – one dose daily for 7 days
Nitric acid 30C – one dose daily for 7 days

Lifestyle:
Release internalized hurt and feelings of not
being able to measure up
Work on feeling adequate
Don't use people for self-interest

Liver and Gallbladder Disorders

Foods to Eliminate:
Fats or bottled oils or oil extracts, processed
oils, mayonnaise or butter
Beef, pork, poultry skin, dairy products and
other animal fat
Caffeine, alcohol, sugar, refined
carbohydrates (flours)
Increase fibre

Daily Nutrients:
Vitamin B12 – 1,000 - 2,000 mcg (sublingual)
Selenium – 200-300 mg
Choline – 500 mg
Olive Oil – 1 tablespoon

Herbs:
Dandelion root, Milk Thistle, Ginger, Black
Radish

Homeopathic Remedies:
Hepatine 1M – one dose daily for 14 days

(all liver conditions)
Nux-Vomica 1M – one dose daily for 7 days
(toxic liver)
Lycopodium 1M – one dose daily for 4 days
(metabolic and/or digestive issues)
Sulphur 1M – one dose daily for 4 days
(fatty liver, cirrhosis)
Staphysagria 1M – one dose daily for 5 days
(suppressed anger)
Hepatitis A or B, 200c – one dose daily for 7
days (hepatitis only)

Flower Essences:
Larch, Tansy, Wild oat, Willow

Lifestyle:
Castor oil packs applied over the liver and
gallbladder area for 4 consecutive nights
every week for 3 weeks (See Appendix)
Liver Flush – see Chapter 7
Lose weight
Vigorous exercise – one hour three times per
week (walking, running, swimming, tennis,
biking)
Learn to make decisions; don't procrastinate
(Gallbladder)
Release and transform anger into self-
healing (Liver)

Libido - Low

Foods to Eliminate:
Caffeine, excess alcohol, milk

Daily Nutrients:
Vitamin E – 400 IU
Vitamin B12 – 2,000 mcg (sublingual)
Liquid Iron – as directed on label

Herbs:
Men - Ginseng, Saw Palmetto, Horny Goat Weed
Women – Damiana, Ginseng, Licorice Root, Royal Jelly

Homeopathic Remedies:
Sepia, 1M – one dose daily for 4 days

Flower Essences:
Crab apple, Evening Primrose, Pink Monkeyflower, Sticky Monkeyflower

Lifestyle:
Lose weight
Start exercising – regularly!
Resolve relationship issues with your partner
Love your body

Menstrual Complaints - PMS, Menopause, Peri-Menopause, Bleeding and Cramping

Foods to Eliminate:
Dairy products, beef, caffeine

Daily Nutrients:
Evening Primrose Oil – 1,000 IU
Liquid Iron – as directed on label (bleeding)
Vitamin B6 – 250 mg
Vitamin E – 400 IU
Magnesium citrate or aspartate – 300 mg twice daily
Phosphatidyl Choline – 1,000 mg at bedtime (insomnia and depression)

Herbs:
Kelp, Blue Cohosh, Black Cohosh, Licorice root, Yarrow (bleeding)

Homeopathic Remedies:
Caulophyllum 30c – one dose daily for 14 days, or as needed (PMS)
FSH 200c – one dose daily for 14 days (all menstrual disorders)
Ovarinum 1M – one dose daily for 14 days (menopause)
Sepia 1M – one dose daily for 7 days (PMS, menopause, prolapsed uterus)
Lachesis 1M – one dose daily for 7 days (menopause)

Lifestyle:
Lose weight – fat cells produce excessive estrogen
Exercise regularly
Support the thyroid and pituitary (see below)
Deal with feelings of shame, anger, feeling powerless, poor female identity and/or lack of purpose
Learn to forgive

Muscle Pain - Chronic Pain, Cramps, Inflammation, Fibromyalgia and Dystrophy

Foods to Eliminate:
Dairy products, beef, potatoes, sugar, soft drinks, fruit, alcohol

Daily Nutrients:
Calcium citrate or Coral Calcium – 2 capsules at bedtime
Magnesium citrate or aspartate – 500 mg

Potassium – 200 mg
Vitamin E – 800 IU
Vitamin B5 – 500 mg
MSM – 2,000 mg
Drink alkaline water (2-3 glasses)

Herbs:
Chamomile, Valerian Root, Wild Yam

Flower Essences:
Dandelion, Crab Apple, Peppermint, Star of Bethlehem

Homeopathic Remedies:
Combination Tissue Salts 6x – Ferr Phos, Kali Sulph, Mag Phos
Arnica 1M – one dose daily as needed
Rhus-tox 200c – one dose twice daily as needed
Gelsemium 200c – one dose twice daily as needed

Lifestyle:
Weight-training for strength
Swimming and stretching for flexibility
Use a Vibration Exercise Machine
Lose weight
Resolve chronic worrying; worrying is like praying for the things that you don't want to have happen

---

Obesity and Food Addictions

Foods to Eliminate:
ALL carbohydrates including grains, flours, sugar and fruit
Emphasize light proteins, legumes and vegetables

Eat a high protein breakfast with no carbohydrates. High protein breakfasts decrease appetite by stabilizing insulin levels for the entire day
Potatoes or sweet potatoes allowed every two or three days

Daily Nutrients:
Probiotics – as directed on label
Magnesium citrate or aspartate – 200 - 400 mg
Vitamin B6 – 200 mg
Alpha-lipoic acid – 100 mg
Chromium – 250 mcg (30 days only)
Olive Oil – 1 tablespoon
Spirulina – 3,000 mg - twice daily

Herbs:
Ashwaghanda, Licorice Root, Psyllium Seed, crushed Flax Seed

Homeopathic Remedies:
Insulin 30C – One dose daily for 14 days
Lycopodium 1M – One dose daily for 4 days

Flower Essences:
Chestnut Bud, Evening Primrose, Milkweed, Pink Monkeyflower, Walnut

Lifestyle:
Regular exercise – both weight-bearing and "cardio"
Use a Vibration Exercise Machine
Check thyroid function
Manage stress – excess cortisol causes weight gain
Get enough sleep
"Feel" and express your emotions instead of eating to mask them

Practice mindfulness - in other words, take the time to acknowledge how things are making you feel – before eating!

Pituitary

Foods to Eliminate:
Caffeine, sugar, dairy products

Daily Nutrients:
Vitamin B6 – 250 mg
Selenium – 200 mcg
Alpha-lipoic acid – 100 mg

Herbs:
Ashwaghanda, Chaste Berry, Fo-Ti, Ginseng, Oregon Grape Root

Homeopathic Remedies:
ACTH 200C – one dose daily for 14 days
Pituitary 1M – one dose daily for 14 days
Hypothalamus 200C – one dose daily for 14 days

Lifestyle:
Relieve stress levels
Heal blood sugar/metabolic issues, thyroid problems and reproductive hormone imbalances – all of which stress the pituitary.

Shingles and Neuritis

Foods to Eliminate:
Sugar, fruit, soft drinks
Emphasize raw greens and green juices

Daily Nutrients:
Vitamin B12 – 2,000 mcg (sublingual)

Folic Acid – 6 mg
L-Lysine – 500 mg
Magnesium citrate or aspartate – 300 mg
Olive Oil – 1 tablespoon

Herbs:
Passion Flower, Yellow Dock

Homeopathic Remedies:
Hypericum 30C – one dose twice daily as needed
Rhus-tox 200C – one dose daily for 7 days
Mezereum 30C – one dose daily for 7 days

Lifestyle:
Release anxieties over family and/or money

Sinus Infections

Foods to Eliminate:
Sugar, dairy products, wheat products, beer, wine

Daily Nutrients:
Vitamin A – 10,000 IU twice daily
Liquid Iron – as directed on label
Zinc citrate – 50 mg twice daily

Herbs:
Goldenseal, Garlic, Cayenne Pepper, Horseradish

Homeopathic Remedies:
Kali Bich 200c – one dose daily for 3 days
Pulsatilla, 200c - one dose daily for 7 days
Sulphur 1M – one dose daily for 4 days

Flower Essences:
Calendula, Evening Primrose, Pink
Monkeyflower,

Lifestyle:
Heal inhalant allergies – "See Allergies –
Inhalant"
Test for yeast – See "Candida Albicans"
(sinus infections are often yeast infections
encouraged by antibiotic prescriptions)
Do Tea Tree/Calendula nasal flushes
Do salt water nasal flushes
Release congested emotions; express
yourself freely
Release guilt
Get in touch with what you want

Skin Disorders - Eczema, Psoriasis, Hives, Rashes and Scabies

Foods to Eliminate:
Sugar, wheat, dairy products, eggs, citrus
fruit, tomatoes

Daily Nutrients:
Vitamin A – 10,000 IU
Evening Primrose Oil – 1,000 IU
Liquid Iodine – 2 - 4 drops
Liquid Iron – take as directed on label
Zinc citrate – 50 mg
Calcium citrate or Coral Calcium – 2 capsules
Selenium – 200 mcg

Herbs:
Internal Use: Milk thistle, Dandelion,
Chickweed, Plantain, Yellow dock, Horsetail
External Use: Calendula, Chickweed, Tea
Tree Oil, Zinc Ointment

Homeopathic Remedies:
Graphites 30c – one dose daily for 7 days
Petroleum 30c – one dose daily for 7 days
Calendula 30c – one dose daily for 7 days
Psorinum 30c – one dose daily for 7 days
Sulphur 30c – one dose daily for 7 days
(Repeat another 7 day course of all of the
above if necessary)

Flower Essences:
Lavender, Pink Yarrow, Yarrow

Lifestyle:
Embrace your emotional sensitivities – it is
okay to "feel" the world and the people in it
Work with feelings of vulnerability
Control your irritabilities

Sleep Apnea

Foods to Eliminate:
All grains, carbohydrates, sugar, fruit
Emphasize a high-protein diet

Daily Nutrients:
Folic Acid – 3 mg
Vitamin B12 – 1,000 mcg (sublingual)
Spirulina – 4000 mg

Herbs:
Flax Seed (crushed)

Homeopathic Remedies:
Ignatia 30c – one dose at bedtime, as needed
Staphysagria, 200c – one dose daily for 5 days

Flower Essences:
Pine, Sage

Lifestyle:
Lose weight
Exercise outdoors
Practice self-forgiveness
Review your attitude toward money – be generous

Sleep Disorders - Insomnia, Nightmares

Foods to Eliminate:
Caffeine, sugar, milk
Test for food allergies and intolerances, especially for children

Daily Nutrients:
Calcium citrate or Coral Calcium – 2 capsules at bedtime
Phosphatidyl Choline – 1,000 – 2,000 mg daily at bedtime

Herbs:
Lemon Balm, Passion Flower, Skullcap, Chamomile

Homeopathic Remedies:
Combination Tissue Salts 6x - Kali Phos, Mag Phos, Nat Mur, Silicea - one dose twice daily, morning and bedtime
Ignatia 30c – one dose at bedtime
Phosphorus 30c – one dose at bedtime
Arsenicum 30c – one dose at bedtime

Flower Essences:
Five-Flower Formula, White Chestnut, Lavender, Chamomile

Lifestyle:
Relaxation exercises for nervous tension - stretching and meditation before bed
Deal with unfinished business
Get closure in relationships
Make peace with the past

Thyroid - Hypo, Hyper and Goiter

Foods to Eliminate:
Caffeine, sugar, wheat, flours, excess carbohydrates
Emphasize a low carbohydrate diet

Daily Nutrients:
Kelp – 1,000 mg
Tyrosine – 500 mg
Vitamin B6 – 250 mg
Selenium – 200 mg

Herbs:
Ashwaghanda, Oregon Grape Root, Lemon Balm

Homeopathic Remedies:
Thyroid 200c – one dose daily for 21 days
Nat Mur 200c – one dose daily for 4 days
Calc Carb 200c – one dose daily for 4 days
Apis 1M - one dose daily for 7-10 days (goiter)

Lifestyle:
Heal blood sugar/metabolic issues and reproductive hormone imbalances – both of which stress the thyroid
Express your feelings
Speak up without confrontation
Be careful with "burn-out"
Learn to receive – not just give

Tinnitus and Vertigo

Foods to Eliminate:
Caffeine, sugar, salt, wheat, dairy products

Daily Nutrients:
Vitamin B12 – 2,000 mcg
Magnesium – 200 mg
Potassium – 300 mg
Folic Acid – 3 mg

Herbs:
Passion Flower
St John's Wort Oil – 2 drops in each ear morning and night

Homeopathic Remedies:
Hypericum 30c – one dose daily for 7 days days (tinnitus)
China, 200c – one dose daily for 4 days (tinnitus and vertigo)
Gelsemium, 200c – one dose daily for 7 days (vertigo)
Cocculus, 200c – one dose daily for 7 days (vertigo)

Lifestyle:
Check your blood pressure
TENS (Transcutaneous Electric Nerve Stimulation)
For vertigo see a physiotherapist who performs the Brandt-Daroff technique
Listen to your inner guidance – what needs changing?

Viruses

Foods to Eliminate:
Sugar, wheat, dairy products
Emphasize raw vegetables and juices

Daily Nutrients:
Vitamin C – 2,000 mg
Beta-Carotene – 50,000 IU
Liquid Iron – as directed on label
Selenium – 200 mcg
Colloidal Silver – as directed on label
Olive oil – 1 tablespoon

Herbs:
Astragalus, Echinacea

Homeopathic Remedies:
Use the specific virus nosode in a 200c – one dose daily for 4 days
(For mononucleosis, hepatitis, or West Nile for example, you would use the homeopathic dilution of that specific virus)

Lifestyle:
Slow down a fast lifestyle
Spend time with yourself
Heal guilt, shame and separation anxiety
Get enough sleep
Get fresh air – viruses hate it!

Warts and Moles

Daily Nutrients:
Vitamin A – 10,000 IU
Zinc citrate – 50 mg
External Ointment:
A paste of castor oil, baking soda and vitamin E oil - blend together and apply twice daily
Homeopathic Remedies:
Thuja 1M – one dose daily for 14 days (warts

and moles)
Causticum 1M – one dose daily for 4 days (warts)
Nitric Acid 1M – one dose daily for 4 days (warts)

Flower Essences:
Goldenrod, Sweet Pea

Lifestyle:
Deal with feelings of not belonging
Find a group that "fits", rather than trying to "fit" into a group

----

Yeast Infections
See Candida Albicans (The Yeast Syndrome)

Important Notes:

Food Notes
Most people who are sensitive to dairy products can tolerate butter in moderation, since butter contains no milk sugar or protein.

Be cautious of possible reactions to gelatin capsules – where possible, empty supplements and herbs into water, juice or soy milk. Capsules can cause a variety of symptoms.

Use alkaline water as sold by commercial water depots; do not use alkalizing drops sold at some health outlets.

Nutrient Notes
Supplements are not meant to be taken over a long period of time. They should be continued only for as long as they are of benefit. This may mean periodically discontinuing all supplements one at a time to determine need. See Chapter 9 for more information.

Iron – Despite the increasing incident of health problems due to high iron levels, the two most common mineral deficiencies in both adults and children continue to be iron and calcium. Symptoms of iron intolerance can include aches, pains, abdominal cramping, headaches and insomnia,

Vitamin C – Use the ascorbic acid form rather than a buffered form such as calcium ascorbate.

Vitamin D - recent research has suggested that Vitamin D is a significant nutrient in the prevention and treatment of a number of diseases, including cancer. Interestingly, in my many years of practice very few people seemed to require it. I maintain that it is a fat-soluble vitamin that, when taken in excess has adverse effects on the cardiovascular system and the immune system. As with all nutrients, take in moderation and test often. Spend lots of time outside, even in the wintertime.

Vitamin E – ensure that it is natural source as indicated by d-alpha tocopherol (not dl)

Zinc – always take zinc with food and for no longer than 30 days.

Herbal Notes
Avoid using echinacea in the presence of auto-immune conditions.

See Chapter 9 for more information on herbs.

Dosages

For herbs listed in this chapter use dosages indicated on the label.

Try not to rely on supplements, herbs or remedies for long-term use. Use as needed only for as long as they are beneficial.

Don't buy combinations of vitamins, minerals or herbs that contain multiple ingredients. Single ingredients allow you to take the exact dosages as suggested or to adjust them later. It also prevents allergy reactions.

Take fish oils in cycles – 3 weeks on and 3 weeks off; this spares the lymph system and the liver from having to process excess oil.

Homeopathy

I have listed specific homeopathic remedies that are of value for the listed health conditions. However, for constitutional prescribing and for a deep-acting remedy with a good fit, it is best to consult with a classical homeopath. See Chapter 9 for more information on homeopathy.

Homeopathic Remedies

One dose = 3 pellets. Let dissolve in a clean mouth. Homeopathic remedies listed for each condition can be taken together unless otherwise indicated.

Flower Essences

Take 4 drops directly out of the stock bottle and into the mouth twice daily – morning and bedtime. (Don't touch your mouth with the dropper).

Medications

If you are taking medication and are concerned with any contraindications check with a knowledgeable and experienced health care provider, herbalist, or nutritional consultant.

Recipe for Good Health

1) Be sure you want to get well: surprisingly - or maybe not - many people have a vested interest in being sick. Remaining ill can help us to get more attention, make our families feel guilty, perpetuate negative emotions, prevent us from having to go to work, make us money (insurance, divorce, settlements), help us to avoid life's realities, and even fulfill a hidden death wish. Have your injuries or illnesses become your belief system? Focusing on illness is a negative mindset – is this really where you want to be?

2) Keep a positive attitude. If you use the following words in your vocabulary on a regular basis to describe yourself, other people, events or stories then you likely have a negative mindset:

NEGATIVE MINDSET WORDS	
• hate	• I don't like
• stupid	• bad
• awful	• wrong
• terrible	• disgusting
• horrible	• hope
• tragic	• disaster
• idiot	• "name-calling"
• frightening	

See if you can get through one day without using any one of these words or similar words. Do it with a friend or an entire family!

3) Hang on to your sense of humour. If you don't have one, get one! Life is fun, fascinating, and full of passion and spirit. Use laughter and joy to heal…every day.

4) Be an optimist – always! Even during hardships and challenges, the outcome is determined by whether or not you regard your problems as an insurmountable difficulty or as an opportunity to improve your life. Focus on what you want rather than on what you don't want or have; you will attract what you focus on.

5) KNOW that you will get well. Don't hope or think that you will – know that you will.

6) Enjoy the healing journey; it's exciting and rewarding. Good health transforms attitudes, builds strong relationships, improves finances and nurtures the spirit. Be patient and appreciate the ebb and flow of life…

All is Light…

Chapter 9

SUPPLEMENTS, HOMEOPATHY and HERBS
- What, When, Why, How -

Nutritional Supplements

Why Are Supplements Necessary?

In an ideal world, adequate levels of vitamins and minerals would be available in the diet to sustain the numerous body functions and processes that support life itself. Were this the case, an adequate diet would be all that is necessary to prevent all nutrition-related (which is most) diseases. However, we must deal with many factors that compromise optimum nutrient levels: processed foods, junk foods, inorganic foods, imbalanced diets, caffeine, alcohol, drugs and medications, environmental toxins, lack of exercise, aging and stress – all of which deplete nutrients. Very often the body becomes so depleted that diet, even a good one, can no longer provide the dosages necessary to regain good health.

Aside from overt symptoms of nutritional deficiencies, sub-clinical nutrient deficits are omnipresent but not commonly identified as the cause of ill health and disease. Nonetheless they have a significant impact on health – especially when corrected!

Therapeutic nutrition goes beyond the prevention of clinical disease, improving health by using optimal levels of specific nutrients including vitamins, minerals, amino acids and essential fatty acids. It is the rare health condition that does not benefit from - or even derive a cure from - applied therapeutic nutrition, which is why it should be considered a primary therapy. I am blessed to have acquired the nutritional knowledge and expertise to help myself and thousands of others whose health problems can very often only be resolved through diet and nutrition.

For how long should supplements be taken? The duration of a health program depends on the specific health condition, as well as on the actual supplements. Positive results and changes are often observed within 1-2 weeks; however chronic problems can take longer. In general, vitamins and minerals should be taken at the recommended dosage for 4 to 6 weeks. After that time, if the condition has improved, continue to take a smaller maintenance dose twice weekly instead of daily. Maintenance dosages prevent deficiencies from reoccurring and also prevent problems from excess. If the original condition reappears on the maintenance dosage, then resume the full dosage as recommended.

It is not advisable to stay on any supplement program indefinitely – whether they are herbs, vitamins, minerals, homeopathic remedies or nutraceuticals. Conditions are always changing and people are always in a state of flux, as it should be. To keep up with these changes, supplement programs should

be re-assessed and/or energy tested on a regular basis. Many people have been taking the same supplements for several months or even years without ever knowing if they are still helping. Taking supplements long-term that are no longer beneficial is detrimental to your health.

As with any supplement, if adverse effects are suspected, discontinue taking the product. The use of kinesiology to determine the benefits and dosages of supplements will prevent most problems or complications.

Homeopathic Remedies

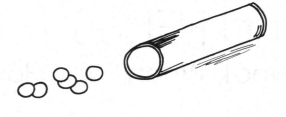

What is Homeopathy?

Homeopathy is a natural system of medicine that uses highly diluted doses of substances to stimulate the body's own healing mechanism. Homeopathic remedies are commonly prepared from plants, minerals or animal products. Also known as "vibrational medicine", homeopathic medicine is based on the principle that natural substances are capable, in a diluted form, of curing the same symptoms that they cause in a crude form when taken by a healthy person. This is known as the Law of Similars or "like cures like".

When a substance is administered in large, crude dosages to a healthy body it will produce specific symptoms of disease, but when this same substance is reduced and diluted to the "essence" of the substance it will stimulate the body's reactive forces to relieve the symptoms and overcome the condition. For example, crude arsenic causes symptoms of poisoning such as vomiting, diarrhea, sweating, restlessness and anxiety, but in minute doses it will actually relieve these symptoms of poisoning. Peeling an onion causes irritating eye and nose discharges, and therefore homeopathic onion is a useful remedy for allergies as well as the common cold.

Why Homeopathy?

Instead of suppressing symptoms, homeopathic remedies support the inherent ability of the body to heal. They are fast acting, effective and extremely safe, with no unwanted side effects. They can be used for people - including babies and the elderly – and animals.

Administering and Storing Homeopathic Remedies

Homeopathic remedies are available as small white soluble sugar tablets, granules or pellets, and in a liquid form which can be added to water. They are also available as ointments or liniments that are used externally. Soluble forms as well as liquids should be administered directly into a clean mouth without food otherwise the vibration may be absorbed by the food. Homeopathic remedies should be stored away from direct sunlight, strong electrical fields such as computers, refrigerators, stoves or other appliances, and aromatic substances such as essential oils. There is no evidence to support claims that the mint family neutralizes the vibration. However, hours spent in front of the computer may do so, as will X-rays, MRI's, CAT scans and other strong magnetic fields when taking homeopathic remedies.

When to Use

Homeopathic remedies can be used for virtually all health conditions including injuries, inflammation, flu, colds, fevers, skin conditions, respiratory problems, allergies, infections, digestive issues, hormonal imbalances, depression, anxiety and other emotional problems. In acute conditions, homeopathic medicines are very fast acting; results are often experienced within one to two minutes of administering the correct remedy.

Homeopathic remedies are usually prescribed for a specific period of time, normally between 3 and 14 days. However, as a general rule, and unless otherwise instructed, discontinue the remedy as soon as symptoms disappear; if symptoms reappear repeat the remedy and continue as needed. On occasion a homeopathic remedy that is taken for too long may bring out symptoms that a person has not experienced before. This is known as a "proving" - it is not serious and the symptoms will disappear as soon as the remedy is discontinued.

A variety of homeopathic medicines are recommended in Chapter 8 for specific health conditions. However, there are many different remedies that can be beneficial for the same health condition. For in-depth and/or constitutional prescribing it is best to consult with a Homeopathic Practitioner.

Therapeutic Herbs

What are Herbs?

Herbal remedies generally consist of dried plants that are powdered, cut and sifted, or have been made into a liquid tincture by soaking the herbs in a water and alcohol solution. Herbs have been used for centuries as foods and medicines; in fact, many common pharmaceutical drugs are made from herbal extracts. However, in natural medicine, the whole plant is used rather than isolating and breaking down the chemical compounds and then synthesizing them, as is done with conventional drugs. The chemical process of synthesis is what produces undesirable side-effects, because the plant has lost all its synergistic properties and is no longer in its original state. Conversely, when a therapeutic plant is used in its whole form it rarely causes side effects. Therefore, it is always better to use the combination of elements as found in plants or herbs - just as nature has provided it – rather than the single chemical within it. Herbs are also of valuable benefit because they are able to address specific body functions or health conditions that cannot be easily resolved in other ways. Detoxification, colon cleansing, blood cleansing, immune-building, hormone balancing, restoring nerves, supporting glands, and energy boosting are just some of the many ways that herbs contribute to good health.

Take herbs as directed for 4-6 weeks. If, after that time, the condition is still gradually improving but not yet resolved, continue taking the herbs. If there is no improvement then discontinue the product. If the health condition has completely improved by that time discontinue the products and see if the condition reappears. If so, then resume the dosage. For chronic problems such as diabetes, heart disease and/or cancer take the herbs for 2-3 months then have someone re-test you with kinesiology. As always, discontinue taking any herb that appears to be causing negative or adverse effects.

While there are hundreds, if not thousands of medicinal herbs, I have in Chapters 6 and 8 listed those that I have found to be of regular clinical benefit for specific health conditions. In this chapter I list a Materia Medica with additional therapeutic information and health benefits for each herb.

Herbal Materia Medica

Aloe Vera

Aloe vera juice is very beneficial for the digestive system. It helps to promote digestive enzymes and has antibiotic and anti-parasitic properties. It's a good digestive cleanser because it absorbs toxins and promotes the growth of probiotics. It has a cooling energy and is very soothing to the mucous membranes and helps to heal intestinal ulcers. Externally aloe vera gel heals burns and wounds.

Ashwaghanda

Ashwaghanda actually means "horse odor", because it smells like a horse. It is an excellent stress reliever and has a marked effect on the endocrine system, particularly the thyroid and pituitary. It will actually help the body increase its own thyroid hormones. It will relieve fatigue and increase vitality and libido. It has mild sedative properties, is a muscle relaxant and boosts the immune system.

Astragalus

Astragalus is a strong immune-enhancing herb with potent anti-viral effects. It has a special affinity for the liver and the lungs, making it a useful remedy for AIDS, hepatitis, liver conditions, colds, bronchitis and chronic infections. It combats fatigue and helps with recovery from chronic illnesses.

Black Radish

Black radish has a pronounced effect on the liver – it stimulates bile flow which acts to detoxify and "flush" the liver and cleanse the blood. All liver toxins are expelled via the bile. It also helps to reduce gravel in the gallbladder. It has a high fibre content that helps to cleanse the colon, thus reducing the flow of toxins that return to the liver.

Black Cohosh

Black cohosh is a female herb that relieves menstrual cramps, spasms and muscle pains. It contains natural estrogen and can be used for hot flashes, nervousness and mental irritability. It combines nicely with Blue Cohosh for a variety of female problems.

Blue Cohosh

Blue cohosh is a gentle female herb that aids with menstrual cramps, spasms and false labour pains. It has a gentle calming effect in cases of pre-menstrual syndrome and menopause, relieving irritability and mood swings. It combines nicely with Black Cohosh.

Chamomile

Chamomile is a soothing nerve tonic with mild sedative properties. It is gentle enough for children and very effective for anxiety, intestinal cramps, colic, teething and insomnia.

Chickweed

This is an amazing little herb that helps to heal ulcers, inflammation and congestion. Combine with Yellow Dock and Plantain to heal almost all skin conditions and to dissolve tumours, growths and sarcoids. Applied externally it makes an excellent poultice for wounds, tumours, boils, abscesses and burns. It will also neutralize the sting after contact with Stinging Nettle.

Comfrey

Comfrey has been used as a healing herb since 400 B.C. I know of no known incident of liver damage in any person who has used comfrey root correctly. (It is also available as a safe homeopathic dilution). As with all herbs, it should be taken temporarily until the condition has improved. Comfrey Root stimulates new cell growth that supports rapid healing of bones and connective tissue. It is therefore known as the "bone knitter" and "bone healer". It can be used for joint inflammation, arthritis and nodules. Comfrey Leaf is beneficial for skin problems, rashes, abscesses, respiratory inflammation and intestinal ulcers.

Dandelion Root

Dandelion induces bile flow, which is how the liver eliminates toxins. It is a liver tonic, blood builder, herbal diuretic and is beneficial for diabetes. Use for anemia, skin conditions, blood and liver conditions, kidney disorders and nutrition. It combines well with Milk Thistle to detoxify the liver.

Dong Quai

This is another female herb with strong hormone balancing properties. It contains natural estrogen and is therefore very useful for menstrual disorders, menopause, hot flashes, mood swings and PMS.

Echinacea

It is likely the most common herb used by North Americans and is widely used for colds and flus. Its main benefit is to improve filtration and drainage of the lymph system, and to purify the blood. It is an antibiotic and anti-viral, stimulates phagocytosis and T-cell formation and expels poisons. Don't use Echinacea if you have an auto-immune condition of any kind. It combines well with Goldenseal as a natural antibiotic and antiviral.

Fo-Ti (Ho-Shou-Wu)

Fo-Ti has a powerful effect on the brain glands - pineal, hypothalamus and pituitary. It therefore acts as a brain tonic improving mental symptoms, fatigue, debilitation and the effects of aging.

Garlic

This has to be one of the most potent herbs in the herbal pharmacy. It is an antibiotic, anti-viral, anti-fungal, anti-parasitic and antioxidant. It stimulates the lymphatic system and helps rid the body of chemicals and heavy metals. It protects against cancer, heart disease, and colds and flus. It should be used as part of any cleansing and/or immune-building program.

Ginger

Ginger is a warm stimulating herb that helps with digestive problems such as gas, bloating, colic, nausea and vomiting. It has pain relieving properties and can be used for cramping, including menstrual cramps. It combines nicely with Garlic for flus, colds and viruses.

Ginseng

The "King of Herbs", ginseng promotes vitality, immunity, energy, libido and stamina. It helps with burn-out, nervous disorders, and mental and physical exhaustion. Use with any health condition where tonic effects are desired.

Goldenseal

Goldenseal has a specific action on mucus membranes as an herbal antibiotic, anti-viral and anti-inflammatory. It also has a tonic effect on the liver and immune system. Use for infections (internal and external), wounds, liver diseases, cancer, skin disorders, gum diseases and nasal and sinus problems. It has a special effect on the lymph system and combines well with Echinacea for lymph problems.

Gotu Kola

Gotu Kola is one of the best brain herbs and

often achieves better results than Gingko. It helps with memory, learning ability and ability to concentrate. It has also been used for mental symptoms and mental fatigue as it increases circulation to the brain. It is an excellent brain tonic that is well tolerated.

Horsetail

Horsetail is very rich in silica and sulphur, making it an excellent choice for skin conditions, urinary problems and recovery from muscle and bone injuries. Horsetail will improve nails, skin, hair, connective tissue and kidney function. Use for 3-4 weeks.

Juniper Berry

Juniper Berry has a tonic effect on the kidneys and on the pancreas. It helps to dissolve kidney stones and sediment, increases the flow of urine and cleanses the blood. It also helps to produce useable insulin, aiding conditions of hypoglycemia and diabetes.

Kelp

A "super-food" from the sea, kelp contains more than 60 trace minerals and numerous vitamins, making it one of the most beneficial foods known. It is particularly high in iodine, which supports the thyroid in metabolic disorders, weight problems and poor immunity. It also has the ability to bind radioactive substances and can reduce the risk of poisoning from environmental pollution.

Lemon Balm

This is a very calming and soothing herb that will treat sleeping problems and nervous ailments. It can also help calm a hyperactive thyroid. It combines well with Passion Flower and Skullcap.

Licorice Root

This is an amazing herb with multiple uses. Licorice root supports the adrenal glands in cases of fatigue, adrenal burn-out and hormonal imbalances of any kind. It is also a mild phyto-estrogen making it useful for menopause. It soothes mucous membranes for asthma, coughs and congestion, and it helps regulate blood sugar levels.

Lobelia

Known as "Indian Tobacco", lobelia is exceptional for the respiratory system. It relaxes the bronchial tubes and will remove disease and congestion from the lungs with asthma, bronchitis and lung diseases. It will also decrease the desire for nicotine when quitting smoking. Combine with Coltsfoot, Horehound and Mullein for an effective lung and bronchial tonic.

Milk Thistle

Milk thistle is one of the most common herbs used for liver detoxification. It is useful for any liver condition: hepatitis; cirrhosis; congestion; fatty liver deposits; poisoning and inflammation. It will also protect the kidneys and brain from chemical toxins. In addition, it will help to block allergy reactions of any kind. It combines well with Dandelion Root for liver detoxification.

Mushrooms

All of the mushrooms have an amazing effect on the immune system.

Reishi is an anti-viral that can be used for viral hepatitis, AIDS and allergies. It has a natural affinity for the respiratory system and can be used for asthma, bronchitis, chronic coughing and after quitting smoking. It acts as a natural anti-histamine, helps to regenerate the liver, reduces heart problems and is a powerful immune-stimulating agent with anti-tumour activity. It has sedative properties reducing stress as a healthy benefit.

Shiitake is one of the best choices for any immune boosting program, including cancer programs. Shiitake is an anti-viral and promotes the immune system to produce interferon, T-helper cells and macrophages. Shiitake is of benefit with every type of cancer. It is often combined with Maiitake, another immune-boosting mushroom, for optimum results with cancer and other chronic diseases.

Oregon Grape Root
Known as the "Herb of the Blood", Oregon Grape Root has value as a blood cleanser, liver detoxifier and will stimulate an underactive thyroid. Use Oregon Grape Root for skin diseases as well.

Passion Flower
It is a good herb for calming the nerves and has special benefit for nervous problems associated with muscle twitching, tics, irritability, poor concentration and epilepsy. It is very well tolerated and has natural side-effects, acting as a pain killer and anti-inflammatory. It combines well with Skullcap and Lemon Balm.

Pau D'arco
Pau D'arco (Taheebo) is a tree from the Amazon. Its main action is on the blood and lymph system as a cleanser, purifier, and immune stimulant. It is therefore an important herb for skin conditions, melanoma, lymphoma, lymph congestion and various cancers. It is also useful for eradicating intestinal yeast and bacteria. It is naturally high in iron.

Plantain
Plantain is the "Mother of Herbs" and is one of the most common herbs in the woods. It is most significant when used as a blood cleanser and skin healer and may also be used as a poultice for wounds, burns, cuts and skin infections. Combine with Yellow Dock and Chickweed to heal skin conditions and to dissolve tumours, growths and sarcoids.

Psyllium Seed
This is one of the best high fibre plants for scrubbing, sweeping and detoxifying the colon as it clings to the intestinal tract, adhering to and cleaning out old putrefied waste material, mal-digested foods and toxins. It also helps to heal "leaky gut". Its fibre has the added benefit of bulking up the stool to resolve both diarrhea and constipation. The seed is more potent than the husk and is less likely to cause bloating.

St. John's Wort
This herb is traditionally used for depression and anxiety, although not everyone can tolerate it. It has a tranquilizing quality that relieves neuralgia, anxiety and nervous

tension. It can also be used for chronic fatigue and burn-out. Positive side effects of St. John's Wort include anti-viral and anti-bacterial properties. It can also heal damaged nerves from physical injury, disease or aging.

Skullcap

Skullcap is a good nerve restorative and helps to rebuild nerve endings. It acts as an effective nerve tonic for sleep, fatigue and anxiety, without having strong sedative or narcotic properties. It combines well with Passion Flower and Lemon Balm.

Slippery Elm

This is one of the most soothing herbs that we can use for healing the intestinal tract. It coats and protects the mucous membranes from toxins and impurities, thus having value in ulcers, Crohn's disease, IBS, colitis, leaky gut or any inflamed or irritated conditions of the intestinal tract.

Spirulina

Spirulina is another amazing "super-food" that is extremely rich in nutrients. It is an excellent source of Beta-carotene, vitamin B12, vitamin B3, calcium, phosphorus, iron and trace minerals. It contains all of the essential amino acids, making it an excellent supplement for vegetarians or those who eat little meat. It is successfully used for weight loss, energy, stamina, detoxification and poor immunity.

Uva Ursi

Uva ursi mainly influences the urogenital system and is traditionally used for bladder and kidney inflammation and prostate problems. It helps to dissolve kidney stones, is a urinary disinfectant and helps the body to rid itself of accumulated acids. It has antibiotic properties and should be used for kidney and bladder infections.

Valerian Root

Valerian can calm all kinds of nervous disorders and has strong sedative effects that act on anxiety, neuralgia, epilepsy, hysteria, spasms, restlessness and migraine headaches. It is also an effective muscle relaxant. However, some people suffer side-effects of depression or feelings of increased hyperactivity; it should therefore be avoided by anyone who is sensitive to it.

Wild Yam

Wild yam is a steroid-like substance that contains a progesterone precursor. Thus, it helps balance conditions of high estrogen levels including weight gain, mood swings and fatigue. It will support exhausted adrenal glands.

Yellow Dock

This is one of the best herbs to use for any skin condition. It cleanses the liver, lymph system and the blood, and has specific action against skin bacteria and parasites. It will help relieve itching, hives, scabies, eczema, rashes and sores. It is high in iron and can be used for anemia. Combine with Chickweed and Plantain to heal almost all skin conditions and to dissolve tumours, growths and sarcoids.

Yucca

Yucca is a natural anti-inflammatory with a

high content of saponins. It acts as a natural steroid which strengthens the adrenals and makes it a very effective herb for joint pain, arthritis, bursitis, skin problems, and allergy reactions. It also has the added benefit of promoting the reproduction of friendly bacteria in the colon.

Appendix A
Illustration of Testing Points

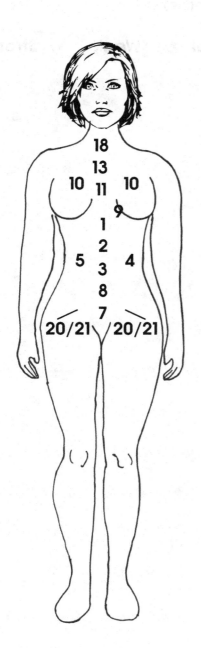

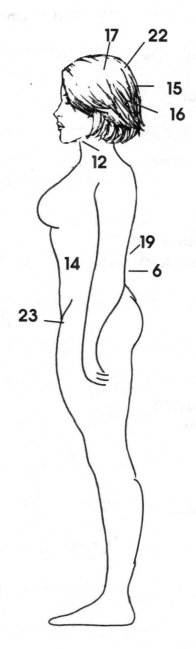

1. Stomach	6. Kidneys	12. Lymph	18. Thyroid
2. Small Intestine	7. Prostate	13. Thymus	19. Adrenals
3. Large Intestine	8. Bladder	14. Spleen	20. Ovaries
4. Pancreas	9. Heart	15. Hypothalamus	21. Testicles
5. Liver &	10. Lungs	16. Pituitary	22. Brain
Gallbladder	11. Bronchials	17. Pineal	23. Blood

Checklist for Testing Organ Points and Body Systems (Use Chapter 6 for a guideline) -

TEST RESULTS	Neutral	Weak	Strong
Gastrointestinal			
Stomach			
Small Intestine			
Large Intestine (colon)			
Pancreas			
Liver			
Gallbladder			
Kidneys & Prostate			
Kidneys (right and left)			
Bladder			
Prostate			
Heart & Lungs			
Heart			
Blood			
Bronchials			
Lungs (right and left)			
Immune System			
Thymus			
Lymph			
Spleen			
Endrocrine System			
Hypothalamus			
Pituitary			
Pineal			
Thyroid			
Adrenals			
Ovaries			
Testes			
Others			
Brain			
Skin			
Bones			
Teeth			
Muscles			
Connective Tissue (ligaments, tendons)			
Protein Levels			
Fat Status			

Appendix C
Advanced Test Points

In Chapter 6 we learned how to test exact organ points and body systems. Chapter 6 also includes a list of advanced test points that can be used by those people who wish to test more details to formulate a comprehensive program.

For example when testing the large colon, you may want to determine what imbalances or underlying problems the colon is dealing with. You may therefore want to test if the colon is suffering from leaky gut, bacteria, yeast, parasites or deficient probiotic levels. In this case you will mentally set your intention on each one of the advanced points being tested and apply one or two fingers to an area on the colon (see illustration of body points). As you are lightly touching the colon area, test the energy of the colon membranes for leaky gut, move your fingers an inch away to another area of the colon and test for bacteria, move your fingers again and test for yeast, and so on. If the muscle test is weak then it is likely that there is an imbalance in the corresponding colon membranes, bacteria levels and yeast levels, etc.

There is no set point on any of these organ areas that anatomically corresponds to the advanced test point. You are determining the point by testing through intention. However, don't apply your fingers to the same area for each test point – always be sure to move your fingers to another area of the organ.

In time and with practice you will become highly intuitive seeing or sensing those points through clairvoyance or clairsentience.

Checklist for Food Allergies and Intolerances

MEAT/PROTEIN

____chicken
____turkey
____beef
____pork
____fish
____shellfish
____eggs
____dairy products
____butter

LEGUMES

____dried beans
____dried peas
____nuts
____seeds
____soy milk
____tofu

GRAINS

____whole wheat (including spelt and kamut)
____white flour (including pasta)
____oats
____rye
____barley
____buckwheat
____millet
____quinoa
____brown rice
____white rice
____bulghar
____flours

VEGETABLES

____artichoke
____asparagus
____beans, green, yellow
____beets
____bokchoy
____broccoli
____brussel sprouts
____cabbage
____carrots
____cauliflower
____celery
____chard
____corn
____cucumber
____eggplant
____garlic
____ginger root
____lettuce
____mushrooms
____onions
____peas
____peppers, green, red

____potatoes
____rhubarb
____spinach
____squash
____sweet potatoes
____tomatoes
____turnips
____yams

FRUIT

____apples
____applesauce
____apricots
____bananas
____blueberries
____cantaloupe
____cherries
____cranberries
____grapes
____grapefruit
____kiwi
____mango
____lemons
____oranges
____peaches
____pears
____pineapple
____raspberries
____strawberries
____watermelon

____dried fruit
____fruit juices

NON-FOODS

____sugar
____caffeine
____chocolate
____margarine
____food additives and preservatives

CONDIMENTS

____salt   ____curry
____pepper   ____mustard

BEVERAGES

____tea, green
____tea, black
____coffee (regular)
____coffee (decaffeinated)
____beer
____wine
____alcohol
____pepsi, coke and pop
____carbonated drinks

Appendix E
Checklist for Vitamins and Minerals

VITAMINS

____Vitamin A
____Beta-Carotene

B-Vitamins
____Vitamins B1 (thiamine)
____Vitamin B2 (riboflavin)
____Vitamin B3 (niacinamid)
____Vitamin B5 (pantothenic acid)
____Vitamin B6 (pyridoxine)
____Vitamin B12 (cyanocobalamine)
____Folic acid

____Vitamin C (ascorbic acid)
____Bioflavanoids
____Vitamin D (cholecalciferol)
____Vitamin E (d-alpha tocopherol)
____Coenzyme Q10
____Alpha-lipoic acid
____Biotin
____Choline
____Inositol

MINERALS

____Calcium   ____Iodine   ____Sulphur
____Magnesium   ____Iron   ____Zinc
____Potassium   ____Silica   ____Copper
____Sodium   ____Chromium   ____Manganese
____Phosphorus   ____Selenium   ____Silver (colloidal)

ESSENTIAL FATTY ACIDS   **NUTRACEUTICALS**

____Fish Oil   ____MSM (methylsulfonylmethane)
____Evening Primrose Oil   ____GLS (glucosaminesulphate)
____Flax Seeds   ____GLHCL (glucosaminehydrochloric acid)
____Lecithin   ____Creatinine Monohydrate
____Phosphatidyl Choline
____Phoshatidyl Serine

Castor Oil Packs

Castor oil packs are a long-forgotten body therapy that are wonderfully soothing and effective for diverticulitis, colitis, constipation, gallstones, liver congestion, scar tissue, growths and tumours. Castor oil has the ability to break up thick tissue, congestive conditions, mal-digested intestinal material and blockages.

1) Prepare a piece of wool flannel cloth (or other suitable material) large enough to cover the affected area. Dampen material with castor oil until saturated but not "dripping".

2) Heat in a 250F oven just until warm. Remove and lay over the affected area. Be careful, the oil can get very hot.

3) Cover with a piece of saran wrap, a towel, and a hot water bottle in that order. Keep pack as hot as is comfortable.

Time: 1 – 1-1/2 hours per session
Frequency: 4 consecutive nights per week for 2 weeks, unless otherwise directed.

Mix together baking soda and water to make a thin paste that can be used to remove excess castor oil from the skin. The pack may be used several times before re-soaking.

Appendix G

Emotional Kinesiology (See Chapter 6)

Emotional States

Abandonment
Abuse
Addiction
Acceptance
Aggressiveness
Alcoholism
Anger
Anxiety
Apathy
Attachment
Attention

Betrayal
Bitterness
Blame
Boredom
Brain trauma
Complaining
Confidence
Control
Courage
Criticism
Cruelty

Defensiveness
Defiance
Denial
Depression
Despair
Disappointment
Discouragement
Dishonesty
Disorientation
Distrust
Domineering
Doubt
Drugs

Ego
Envy
Failure
Faith
Fear
Forgiveness

Frustration
Greed
Grief
Guilt
Habit Patterns
Hatred of self
Hatred of others
Hopelessness
Impatience
Inadequacy
Injustice
Inner Child
Intimacy
Intolerance
Insecurity
Irritability

Judgement
Laziness
Loneliness
Love
Martyrdom
Masochism
Materialism
Morality
Negativity
Non-attachment

Obsession
Oversensitivity
Overwhelm
Panic
Paranoia
Perfectionism
Pessimism
Possessiveness
Power
Prejudice
Pride

Rebelliousness
Religion
Repression
Resentment
Resistance

Responsibility
Revenge

Sadism
Sadness
Secrecy
Selfishness
Self-esteem
Self-image
Self-punishment
Self-worth
Sentimental
Separation
Sexual distress
Shock
Sympathy
Shame
Stubbornness

Terror
Trauma
Violence
Vulnerability

Personal Relationships

Wife
Husband
Ex-wife
Ex-husband
Mother
Father
Son
Daughter
Brother
Sister
Uncle
Aunt
Grandfather
Grandmother

Friend
Neighbour
Business Associate
Co-Worker

Teacher
Leader
Mentor
Family group

Higher self
Higher guide
Angel
Discarnate
Religious group
Church
Other groups
Supreme Being such
as God (or any deity
worshiped)

Times or Places

Alternate/other life
Parallel universe
Death
Bardo
Current event
Future event
Past events
   - Conception
   - Birth
   - Womb
   - Infant
   - Childhood to
age 12
   - Teenager
   - Age 20's
   - Age 30's
   - Age 40's
   - Age 50's
   - Age 60's
   - Age 70's
   - Age 80's

(If you're older than
90 congratulations
you don't need to be
reading this book, you
need to be writing
it).

List for Testing Diets and Cleanses

LIST of DIETS

1) Paleolithic #1 (Caveman and Cavewoman) – no sugar, no grains, no dairy products, no legumes

2) Paleolithic #2 (Caveman and Cavewoman) – no sugar, no grains, no dairy products, no legumes, but no beef

3) Atkins Diet Program #1 – low carbohydrate, high fat, high protein

4) Atkins Diet Program #2 – low carbohydrate, high fat, high protein but no beef or dairy

5) Seafood, Fruit and Vegetables

6) Seafood and Vegetables (no fruit)

7) Vegetarian #1 – whole grains, legumes, vegetables, fruit

8) Vegetarian #2 – whole grains, legumes, vegetables (no fruit)

9) Vegetarian #3 – rice only, legumes, vegetables, fruit

10) Vegetarian #4 – rice only, legumes, vegetables (no fruit)

11) Raw Food Diet - with cooked meat for protein

12) Raw Food Diet – with nuts and seeds for protein (no meat)

13) Calorie Counting – 2400 calories/ day; 2100 calories/day; 1800 calories/day; 1500 calories/day; 1200 calories/day

14) Low Fat – no fats, no extracted oils, low fat meats, low fat foods

15) Grapefruit and Egg Diet

16) Gluten and Dairy-Free Diet

17) Low Acid Diet – avoid acetic, citric, arachadonic, phosphoric and oxalic acids.

18) Food Combining – Do not combine meat with grains. Do not combine citrus fruits with grains.

19) Alternating Paleolithic Diet #1 with Vegetarian Diet #1 (in 2 to 4 day cycles)

20) Candida Program – no sugar, wheat, dried fruit, caffeine, beer or wine

LIST of CLEANSES

21) Master Cleanse – maple syrup, lemon juice, cayenne pepper, water 3 day, 7 day or 10 day

22) Grape Juice Diet – white grape juice or purple grape juice

23) Vegetable Juice Fast – carrot, celery, beet, parsley, spinach, cabbage, tomatoes

24) Three Day Apple Fast

25) Liver Flush – olive oil, lemon juice and castor oil packs

Recommended Reading

Adam. Dreamhealer His Name is Adam. Canada: DreamHealer.com. 2003.

Adam. Dreamhealer 2. Canada: DreamHealer.com. 2004.

Atkins, Robert. Dr. Atkins New Diet Revolution. New York, New York: Harper Collins. 2002.

Brandt, Johanna. "The Grape Cure". New York: Ehret Literature Publishing Company. 1971.

Brandt, Johanna. "How To Conquer Cancer Naturally". Tree of Life Publishing. 1996.

Boericke, W. Homeopathic Materia Medica and Repertory. New Delhi, India: B. Jain Publishers Ltd. 1998.

Burroughs, Stanley. The Master Cleanser with Special Needs and Problems. Reno, NV: Burrough Books. 1993.

Carper, Jean. The Food Pharmacy. New York: Bantam Books. 1988.

Carr, Alan. Easy Way to Quit Smoking. Oakville, Ontario: Clarity Publishing. 2004.

Castro, Miranda. Homeopathic Guide to Stress. Great Britain: Pan Books. 1996.

Castro, Miranda. The Complete Homeopathy Handbook. London: Macmillan London Limited. 1991.

Chapman, J.B. Dr. Schuessler's Biochemistry. London, England: New Era Laboratories. 1975.

Cordain, Loren. The Paleo Diet: Lose Weight and Get Healthy By Eating the Foods You Were Designed to Eat. Hoboken, New Jersey: John Wiley & Sons Inc. 2002.

Dyck, Agneta. Why I Canceled my Health Insurance. Guadalajara, Mexico. 2011.

Epstein: Gerald. Healing Visualizations. New York, New York: Bantam Books. 1989.

Erasmus, Udo. Fats and Oils. Vancouver, B.C.: Alive Books. 1986.

Gagne, Steve. Food Energetics. Rochester, Vermont: Healing Arts Press. 2008.

Gawain, Shakti. Creative Visualization. Berkeley, California: Nataraj Publishing. 1995.

Gibson, Douglas. Studies of Homeopathic Remedies. Bucks, England: Beaconsfield Publishers Ltd. 1991.

Harling, Marianne and Kaplan, Brian. Studies of Homeopathic Remedies. Bucks, England: The Homeopathic Trust. 1991.

Hay, Louise. You Can Heal Your Life. Santa Monica, CA: Hay House, Inc. 1984.

Karp, Reba Ann. Edgar Cayce Encyclopedia of Healing. New York: Warner Books. 1986.

Kaminski, Patricia and Katz, Richard. Flower Essence Repertory. Nevada City, California: The Flower Essence Society. 1996

Kirschmann, Gayla and Kirschmann, John D. Nutrition Almanac. New York: McGraw-Hill. 1996.

Murphy, Robin. Homeopathic Medical Repertory. Pagosa Springs, Colorado: Hahnemann Academy of North America. 1993.

Ritchason, Jack. The Little Herb Encyclopedia. Pleasant Grove, Utah: Woodland Health Books. 1995.

Vitale, Joe. The Key. Hoboken, New Jersey: John Wiley & Sons, Inc. 2008.

About Marijke

Marijke van de Water holds a B.Sc. in Clinical Nutrition and a Diploma in Homeopathic Medicine and Science. She has been in private practice for over twenty years as a gifted and widely respected healer. She started her early career counseling people in holistic clinical nutrition - nutrition has always been a major passion for Marijke as she observed that the results of many other health therapies were often stalled or limited by the adverse health effects of unidentified food intolerances and/or nutrient deficiencies. Conversely, there were also people whose nutritional programs were in order but their health still did not progress. At this point, recognizing the need for more healing modalities, Marijke acquired her Degree in Homeopathy as well as continuing to develop her practice in Kinesiology, Energy Medicine and Medical Intuition. Marijke became and continues to be a knowledgeable and highly sensitive medical intuitive with an uncanny ability to perceive the true and underlying cause of many health and medical conditions.

Then, after years of extensive experience, and with the help of feedback from thousands of clients, she developed *The Marijke Method*™, a unique and specialized method for customizing comprehensive and individual health programs. This method identifies the underlying physical, emotional and/or spiritual causes and then corrects them using the appropriate diet, nutrients, herbs and/or energy medicines specifically indicated for that particular person. In this way, the assessments are based on the individual biochemistry and "blueprint" of each person.

As an instructor she presents classes and workshops in Clinical Nutrition, Kinesiology, and Animal Communication as well as facilitating a variety of Healing Retreats. Her expert knowledge, exceptional communication skills and easy style have put her in high demand as a featured speaker at seminars and conferences.

Marijke is also an avid horse-woman who loves animals. She enjoys riding and interacting with her horses through fun-filled horsemanship, soul communications and good food. She is well-known in the equine health industry and is also the author of *Healing Horses: Their Way!* and is the founder of Riva's Remedies, an equine herbal and homeopathic product line distributed across North America. (www.rivasremedies.com)

Through this book - *Healing People: The Marijke Method*™ - it is Marijke's most sincere and heartfelt desire to share her practical healing techniques and her common sense wisdom to make the world a brighter, happier and healthier experience for all people.

For Information on Seminars, Workshops,
Conference Presentations,
Health Products and Books:

www.marijke.com
www.rivasremedies.com
Phone: 1-800-405-6643

Other Books by Marijke van de Water:

Healing Horses: Their Way!
Sapphire Publishing, October 2008